POST-PRAIRIE

POST-PRAIRIE

AN ANTHOLOGY OF NEW POETRY

Edited by

Jon Paul Fiorentino & Robert Kroetsch

Talonbooks

Vancouver

Talonbooks
P.O. Box 2076, Vancouver, British Columbia, Canada V6B 3S3
www.talonbooks.com

Typeset in Adobe Garamond and printed and bound in Canada.

First Printing: 2005

The publisher gratefully acknowledges the financial support of the Canada Council for the Arts; the Government of Canada through the Book Publishing Industry Development Program; and the Province of British Columbia through the British Columbia Arts Council for our publishing activities.

LIBRARY AND ARCHIVES CANADA CATALOGUING IN PUBLICATION

Post-prairie : an anthology of new poetry / edited by Jon Paul Fiorentino & Robert Kroetsch.

ISBN 0-88922-523-0

1. Canadian poetry (English)—21st century. 2. Canadian poetry (English)—Prairie Provinces. 3. Prairie Provinces—Poetry. I. Fiorentino, Jon Paul, 1975–
II. Kroetsch, Robert, 1927–

PS8295.5.P7P68 2005   C811'.60809712   C2005-902459-3

Dedicated to the memory of Marvin Francis

CONTENTS

POST-PRAIRIE POETICS: A DIALOGUE

Since myth robs language of something, why not rob myth?
—Roland Barthes

Robert Kroetsch and I wanted to document and celebrate the poetry of the prairie as it is being written now, in the new century. We soon discovered that the prairie was missing, or perhaps the prairie had become in many ways unrecognizably present in this new work. The poets we have gathered here (both poets of the prairie and poets of the prairie diaspora) are speaking in new voices, and their "home place" of the prairie has become less unified, more urban, technologically adept, and theoretically informed. To put it another way, the "home place" is where it's not: there are elements of a vernacular inclusion project in this anthology. The inability of many readers and literary scholars to see an emerging poetics of a new prairie, the post-prairie, should not be surprising—there is a reason the prairie is thought of as the domain of the rural, the wheat field and the grain elevator. This most obviously has something to do with its history, but the persistence of this imagery also has something to do with cultural capital—that is, there is a marketplace-based reason many people continue to think of the prairie as a fixed notion of "traditional" landscape. Perhaps it's easier to sell the prairie as such a simple place, located in some past golden page of a "simpler" life. In order to desimplify this notion, to figure out what we were getting at by gathering the elements of this anthology, where we were getting to, we, the editors, needed to dialogue.

§

RK: The question for me is this: What is the new surround for these new poets? You see what I mean? They are immersed, but in what? Where in hell did the prairie get to? How do these new poets reshape context?

JPF: *Post-Prairie* is a collection of descriptive poetic grammar. These are poets who unwrite the prairie. I suppose it is not enough to say they are immersed in immersion. The idea of descriptive poetics (as opposed to prescriptive) is key. Look at beaulieu's meta-descriptive exercise entitled "pronoun woven." Here is a text that serves as a multi-layered scholarly/poetic endeavour. Further, he reshapes the context by beginning on the streets. Where, specifically in hell, did the prairie get to? I think it's still here/there but the poets are elsewhere, or hiding, or resisting. The anxiety of geography is reshaping the context.

RK: Okay, let me put it another way, what is the new obsession? I'm thinking of your Transcona poems as a place to begin. My obsession was silence itself, as it might be for Doug Barbour. Consider Doug's work with the overflow of bpNichol as a cover for his own creating of gaps. But tell me about these new vocal folds (I hear "chords" has been replaced by "folds") and the beautiful noise they are making. And without inhibition.

JPF: My obsession is with the performance of place, of not remaining true to place, and finding that the fictive is just as "true." Maybe there is something here: for me, Transcona is an interesting geographic symbol—it was a prairie town, and Winnipeg grew around it and swallowed it. However, no one should begin with my Transcona poems. I turn to the poetry and criticism I had discovered within and without the prairie. And I am far from alone in terms of my influences. One might say that this is a collection of poets under the influence.

RK: I'm a firm believer in influence. Under the influence, okay, but of what?

JPF: The connotative overflow of your *Seed Catalogue*, Cooley's *Fielding*, Wah's *Waiting for Saskatchewan*, and Van Herk's "Calgary, this growing graveyard," to name a few influential texts; critically speaking, the influence of Dennis Cooley's remarkable essay, "The Vernacular Muse in Prairie Poetry," is clear. If the previous prairie ethic/aesthetic relied on notions of found linguistic material (as opposed to received linguistic material), of an extrapolation of vernacular (as opposed to idiom), of reproaching universality (as opposed to approaching universality), then this project necessarily becomes an extension of that ethic as well as a response. Cooley muses that "it must be difficult, even for the curious, not to perceive vernacular poetry as a failure of imagination or intelligence" (171). The reception of poetry has, for the most part, always relied on an implicit anti-vernacular notion to inform its status as a "high cultural act." Cooley stresses the importance of the subjective, regional, marginalized voice within the poetic process. The struggle for respectability is evident throughout Cooley's essay; but a corresponding awareness of the nature of such struggles is evident as well. For Cooley, transgressive acts are necessary in the establishment of a new poetics. Critical theory is alive in many of these poets' texts, as it is in Cooley's and yours.

RK: Cooley is of two minds in a fascinating prairie Saskatchewan CCF way. He disowns the symbolic, but when he sees the word light he sounds like Tommy Douglas. But then he goes right from that to his Robin Hood sympathies for the murderous Bloody Jack. The space in between is the dark matter that contains the prairie poems of his generation. Cooley is the model in turmoil.

JPF: The model is turmoil is Cooley. The political ethic is still there. Rob Budde's "SOFTWARE TRACKS" is very much an exercise in thinking against the discourse of "high art" poetry and notions of universality through the implementation of a Steinian model of syntax. Budde presents us with the following possibility: "It could be the code is broken," and this canonical distrust is ever-present in the post-prairie modality. We have reached a point where the postmodern work pioneered by such texts as Cooley's has served to re-define what is permissible within the realm of "high art" poetry. Canonical value has since been assigned to many of the poems of Cooley's prairie poetry project. What *The Vernacular Muse* teaches us is that we must be ever-vigilant regarding the processes of ascribing literary value. We must question official poetry language. We must catch ourselves when we slip.

RK: Linguistic structures create us as much as we create them. Or more so, I would guess, as Roy Miki argues, and he is a prairie poet (Ste-Agathe and Winnipeg). How do these young pups wiggle out of that one?

JPF: In a recent article entitled "The Prairies as Cosmopolitan Space," Jason Wiens claims that "if we examine historically how prairie poetry has been framed, constructed and championed in academic discourse, we can discern consensus on certain critical points." The championing of prairie poetry as a rural domain needs to be troubled. Wiens asserts that by troubling consensus, prairie critics and poets can move toward "fluidity" and therefore articulate and antagonize the received poetic tradition (162). It occurs to me that this is the cultural work that the post-prairie poem is engaged in. There is an anxiety of geography at work in the post-prairie poem. It longs for its home, only to "trouble" the very articulation of home. The urban lyric world of Chandra Mayor, who sings of Winnipeg as "a misshapen city ... tied up by the perimeter like a noose," denotes a shift toward the cosmopolitan space, toward a strange, contingent universality, still tethered to the home place, even as it antagonizes.

RK: Place is where it's at.

JPF: I'm with you. Any regional classification hinges on problematic assumptions of a monolithic nature. Deborah Keahey states that "beginning to understand the ethos of place, the ways we place ourselves in relationship to geographical spaces, requires demystifying and particularizing our accounts of it" (161). While Keahey makes clear the trappings of such totality, she also points to its functionality. Specificity (in terms of vernacular and cultural locality) is a mode of descriptive grammar. It is in this way that the post-prairie poem is most explicitly an extension of the prairie poem. The post-prairie text recentralizes the home place. The relationship between post-prairie and prairie poets is constructively dialogic. Increasingly urban, the post-prairie poem is both an aesthetic response to the homesteads of the past and a socio-economic reality which reflects the death of the family farm and the establishment of a more cosmopolitan landscape. Now there exists pothole-ridden streets, urban tenements, and images of gentrified homes. The "prairie proper" is now the periphery, and the centre is plural: urban narrative, L=A=N=G=U=A=G=E, the subjective and subjunctive/optative lyric, the renegotiation of modernist points of departure.

RK: The centre is plural. Shit, we old dogs knew that on day one. Let me try again: Are these new poets hearing the city? The sound, Jon. How does the sound change? Tell me about the new sound you so eloquently hear.

JPF: Consider the resonance of your desire to "let the city write itself." Is not the collective desire of these poets to move beyond language analogous to your desire? Many of these texts are sonically charged; the phonetic nature of the poems is often (but not exclusively) urban. And this is why I must stress that plurality. It may not be new, but I think it may have a wider swathe. Wiens would say it is "more fluid"— whether we are discovering the playful homophony of Louis Cabri's "Salon, salon" or Mayor's brilliantly reluctant lyricism. The city in Laurence's "North Main Car" is not Mayor's Winnipeg; but in both cases, the city writes itself. In other cases like Cabri's, field composition is still the practice, but the theory and its articulation are new. Is this how one finds home?

RK: You've been found out. You know what I mean?

JPF: I suppose what has changed is what is found. The poets in this anthology are not working with found material in the same way that Cooley's poets are. In fact, they have received a tradition of Prairie writing from poets such as yourself, Marriot, Mandel, Arnason, Cooley, Suknaski, Wah, and Szumigalski. This tradition of reluctant "home-making" has created a desire in these emerging poets to depart from it, or dispose of it in a mode which could tangibly be called meta-reluctance. The linguistic material of the post-prairie poet is more strikingly urban, displaced, resistant of the now canonical prairie vernacular or hyperbolically insistent on a kind of hyper-vernacular, or dependent on a desire to democratize vernacular—to include the urban "other" of the region, dedicated to a resituated centrality. What post-prairie poets are finding is that the task of establishing a home place has been achieved for them; but the established home place may be very far from home. The post-prairie poem: a found of sorts— revised, resituated, not quite stable.

RK: Yes, I think of the terrors underneath the attempt at stability in the poetry of Lorna Crozier. She is the located dislocated prairie poet, the link/break between was and is, the quiet clamour in the bust-up of the ego's I. What she is unnerved by is the voice faltering its way into voices plural. And all this complicated by her baldheaded-prairie expat condition as she resists and absorbs rainforest anxieties.

JPF: This collection has its share of displaced prairie poets (and I am not just referring here to those who remain on the prairie). Darren Wershler-Henry is singing his post-prairie song (a heavy, heavy metal song) from downtown Toronto.

RK: And ironically the newest among the new is a new version of the old: the aboriginal voice gone urban in bizarre prairie versions of what urban is, European traces dissolved into Winnipeg, country & western learning post-industrial clang.

JPF: Marvin Francis, Rosanna Deerchild, and Duncan Mercredi are essential poets and essential to the success of this book. Francis was an insurgent, a shit-disturbing trickster; Deerchild, amid all of the displacement of this collection, manages to articulate the ironic staticity of the northern town with a stunning lyric voice; Mercredi gives us the gift of his blues riffs, unapologetically urban.

RK: Your stubbornly attentive eye, Jon, makes this anthology the real and precise news, the underwater trumpet blast, the lightning-ravaged tree.

§

Our anthology is part of a growing project. (The prairie is still arable.) The aim of *Post-Prairie* is plural: it is not to dispose of but to resituate the aesthetic that governs poetry of the Canadian prairie. This is not essentialist poetics. This is a poetics of locality and dislocality. The poems that follow often enact a striking resistance to the reductions of the "home place"; at times this resistance is informed by a reverent surrender to the importance of the prairie tradition; at times there is no such reverence. Home is being abandoned and desired here. Poets are calling home; poets are being called home. Some are listening; some are singing too loudly; all are singing the political. This is the first collection of twenty-first-century post-prairie poetry.

Jon Paul Fiorentino and Robert Kroetsch
Montreal / Winnipeg, April 22, 2005

WORKS CITED

Cooley, Dennis. "The Vernacular Muse in Prairie Poetry." In *The Vernacular Muse: The Eye and Ear in Contemporary Literature*. Winnipeg: Turnstone Press, 1987.

Keahey, Deborah. *Making It Home: Place in Canadian Prairie Literature*. Winnipeg: University of Manitoba Press, 1998.

Wiens, Jason. "The Prairies as Cosmopolitan Space: Recent 'Prairie' Poetry." In *Toward Defining the Prairies: Region, Culture, and History*, edited by Robert Wardhaugh. Winnipeg: University of Manitoba Press, 2001.

DEREK BEAULIEU

SUMMER TRIANGLE

four southern regions

rocks leave their own images levels allow left
& left & the & the mad dash *em* or a single
feather

birdman points to one grotto

up is hard down is easier chronically horse

a laugh unabashedly wishing several flights
up for relief

ability to claim space timing the
constellations the sun

map constellations the bird-stick meridian
columns with both feet enter the building
reclaim friendship strong shorter length
surprise on street lost scarf late

struggle with various vertebrae map
cosmology

shapes & feathers

PRONOUN WOVEN

fr. Erin Mouré reading Lisa Robertson

those streets amid opacity she & Robertson heard.
                    the situation's back on poetry
                                        silent green mimesis
              This work beckons—just no hero

         hear the reddened earth so directly
                                        walk—mimic Dante's descent
                    like folded laughter
                                        perpetual braids of ships the brown funnelling
                                        smoke
                                        sob (as in comedy)

                    heard ornament
                              (but a chorus is
pronoun—a woven disjunct of

         fold cupidity yellow—
                                        Pope wrote & Robertson heard.

              so directly—
                                        "I am the grey woods that propel semantic leaps"

    exhaling to explain orchards or made water

    not the individual but criticism (that rhyming boy)

         so we claim itself
                              thinged into tenderness.

         never forgets wit & pleasure.

         elevated tones & barbed words

                              blurred characters stand
                              rote

exhaling itself names things into being
    all barbed words

    not for the motion of slow ships
                          (these burn / so pendant in
   work engages subjectivities
pronoun woven from perpetual braids of flesh

                   life (again).
   let orchards explain orchards
   echoes roll decasyllabic lines
   playful, jauntily new
   .

   individual as criticism
        smoke on lurid water
          just esteem,

                             Annus Mirabilis indeed

   urban courts aphoristic phrasings

   Though she claims

   Like those streets amid opacity

       Most rules are named "pronoun."

   styles & dictions,

   tenderness
   woven so to speak,

   nouns adjust so directly—

   book-length poem
   she claims

so rapturously plucking
       being (an) indispensable
       press of age.

Debbie, too, does this.

             line breaks like verse.
                Like.

ROBERT BUDDE

from *SOFTWARE TRACKS* (2005)

ANOREXIA

Doubled, this hedge-like structure should be trimmed unevenly through acupuncture dismissals. Perusing a periphery. A Jacobean development: after-the-fact but so much more cocktails. Expectantly, custard takes on the spoon, calls for a sudden, an exacting conjunction.

Walking is walking over.

The zipper was.

Window frame spillage, beading, the bones wary even over cotton weave. A relenting. Whoop whoop.

Alibi in stitches.

Litmus line.

A swindle refusing lack. Ignore the next one.

Carousel jargon accounting for the iconoclasm, accounting for the jury pillage. Sameness in an uprising; that radical package deflation. Some say it would never sharpen. The best medicine is a nerve not above believing. Caramel. Staggering the imprint printed precisely because it is not impressionable. Off off. Ten-gallon "récitatif." At the door, the officer showed his required.

Sandstone, stalactite, diction not combining.

Unlike teflon.

Evasions yes evasive no. Of competency that would take one place other than sauces of success. The high highway. Missing that lover who simply. Marked on the script of immigration there was an intravenous moment. A different alphabet meaning yes, there is no arm done.

It could be the code is broken but more likely.

BRUISE

Choreographed escape a charged resolve to repel the hour. Grape leaving that is not wound around. One turns to disservice again but for luck. Utter survival burned in engravings, givens; letting loose without reprisals it could be said. Under garland, under oath. Exhibit this above sugar, or other condiments of power, above brunch as the very last time.

Tempered, the tide or such things, haunt long after the burnt umber, long after the farewell breeze, long after long. Hindsight, charismatic and sure.

Cushions buttering and water overdone. That heavy-lidded smoky smoke. Distinction made air within air. No surface, no claim.

A coronation.

None more than denial of depth.

BODILESS

A deserted syntax gears up absolute.
A hardwood assemblage.
A cyclone surge even after.
Once inhabited, automation and random growth send unregistered waves. Back.
Paths, comets; no expectations.
Typing typing typing typing typing.
As if a voodoo doll could. As if an invocation can. As if the interrogative enters. As if four directions is enough.
Online, the line.

STITCH

Ecstatic conditioning—indexing anatomy.

Eyeclip and radical endorsements.

Upon the discovery of a twin there is a faint thrum of artificially flavoured revulsion. A theory dismissed.

To vex.

The riding crop dropped, the reigns held loosely, a plunge into new arts.

The contemporary narrative that is not beyond and its cohorts all ingested the purchase and the stock. There is no concern here.

The sense of yearning when it is too.

Cantaloupe clearly eaten by the canal as a bridled courtesy. Everything stops at the incisive moment when the dissolved. The end of the story remained over. Effigies re-assemble, are dismissed. A movie inserted under the knee for durable sentences. For every occasion, a pre-ordained violence to ensure patrons. This is about signs about. A chorus of glass decanters and the means by which. Unplugged.

Excursions by canine intuition into.

GAG

Awe showing up before the curtain. A father's pedigree. Blue stripe. Backpacking the path's width. Constructions of space might seem endless but the door.

A shy dip, a tiny furrow.

Arguably there was none.

Where stairs meet landing transitions become a miss.

A lull in the columns.

A pronoun could be here.

Escalators in language produce no agreement and joy.

One had to follow.

After thought, a reconsideration.

Forefinger leading. A tiny resolute fingering, a burrowing unto need, a substantial requirement unrequited. A sum.

Again. Cords reeling change the measure by up and down but not as much by not repeating. A round blueness can counter the most unwieldy of occasions.

A shiny furrow, a shy flip.

These is no reason to say there was a chime, a calling, it was hardly fast and surely soft. There is no pleasure in remarking.

The chin in finishing, in pinning the last cinnamon pastry, in winning the least chuck.

TATTOO

Crosswalk or neighbourhood watch, the shape and colour of habit. An index to
paper pages though hitting the key twice may mean a jurisdictional conflict. Acid-free
oracles bound to end up a propensity to open one's wallet with aplomb.

Forgetting that clothes are on.

Evenly spreading a fanciful indulgence, even though the table is not set nor ever
will. Icons change hands. Wistful thinking leading the rooms of art to the sign
reading "You are her."

A seagull in a mirror requires architectural funding.

Evidence of matter needed.

Therefore, the exhibit was dismantled and all the merchants outraged. A note for
immediacy carries on. A claw in hand might produce a reasonable succession of
events.

The way marks are always.

The company maximizes profit by not requiring. Those things, trembling objects,
in which a collecting does not waylay anyway.

A writing away to.

Dignitaries design, or rather placebo.

Taking on the champion receives numerous; of course this is a prelude to
elevations above air.

Not underground but in between time.

History used as kindling.

A browser hit.

LOUIS CABRI

SALON, SALON

           hacks   with traps

                                             ... I came back

   Wait ... There's a page missing.
   Hey you should put that in your poem!

           Your saying it
           is interesting in every way
           except the verbal?

           Except it, then

                   bring the world.

                                 *

               Are you in one?
               How will you know?

                   On the other hand, for that "other" hand is You (too)—are so
                   spherical to me, don't you see, like Plato imagined, you're
                                                             infinitely
                   reticulated by satellite & optic cable—

                   complete, skin
                   surface, approximate—twenty square feet; dust
                   90% you. Leaf? Yea ... Harbour? Plane? Of course ...

et cetera. Nothing has changed
aver it, except
the will to change.

Except it, then …

"To Bermuda!"

"ME   FUSTIAN"

*

The irony is *stuffed*
—Can't bill some body for it?

stiffed. death*pick*able—Daffy Duck sense
                "what they represent" …

        "Pull down, pull down" …
                        what *we* represent
                                (down, tears,
                                        down!)

                "What

                me, cauliflower?"

                        Frying pantheists, atman!

*

"neither is *ornament* unnatural" (emph. added) …
                muzak über lawn
                lambs open house   "Hegemony is"
                                          Lemony Snicket's
                                                    hedge

                        property is
                        "cute"
                                          literary
                                                    these few lines

all it takes

                                                    Sun for

                                                    What zucc.
                                                    Weight lb.
                                                    Where sill.

                        —I can't look
                                At you be
                                        Cause I have
                                                To read this
                                                        How bob semiotic

                Activity intro
                        Duces wandering
                                Fuzziness into
                                        Language *a*
                                                Fortiori poetic??

        —Excessively
                —Rhetorical
                        —Overloaded
                                —Connotation
                                        —Blur

Takes it—All

                             the world's
        unspeakably   *la demarche*

        body craves

        a tumult   a
    Tastefully interior?

                                       blowhole.

      inside of an inside joke, The

                          *

      Soft humanist lighting
      ethnocentric drapes
          Porcelain bowl
          & golden ... bait (golden apes)

      Says no pots outside ("leopard-skin" clause)—

                "D'oh!"
                       (see dictionary)

            Must ... find ... oxygen ...

Sound-of-falling game:
    gumballs (supermarket aisle),
      gym bags—

Kickboxing car ports
    (after movie)—"They're just
        letting you know ...

      reference

      that reference

      narrates."   —that rather than
                       deferral ("Garbled!")—
                       "this"

                       "Back
                       to you ... " the eyeless
                       back to you; Anyway ...

             ... publicity ... now ...

        "Preference"
        over deference,
      much the 20C
      American

Consumer! look!

To Thy Catalogues & Manuals

            *

Aaaaaalll night
he was a Young Hegelian.
Young Hegelian!

"conservative Christian anarchist," Henry—
from the Adams's family
in which statesmanship is preserved by propagation—something a colour in the leaf of the
Begonia, perpetuating resemblance through perpetual change …
to The Addams Family—

elevation
to *elevator*!
reference to
manual; works to—

The Games

Logos to
logos
DO iT! Scenarios of the Revolution to Just do it.
—My daemon says
Tetley!
"We grant you life,"
Socred tease

(Only in Canada, you say?)

*

Pejorocrats
have thinned ye, Society
        bunged prune;
        Olson in a teacup
                icon

                        Vane

                        Chest wind

                        Control tower

                Get on
                (vocative case)
                download

        Hasslefree impedance
        system w/ adjusting
        "Hefnerism," "Hussainism"—sampling
        world echoes

purloined
integument.
The just
gut noticed

        eviction
        signs.   bruises etc.
                "Bruce's 'etcetera ... '"

                        vs.

"Here

to repair my own cue … "

"Repair to my own cue?"

Water, please … (sound of flushing toilet)
He standeth as Tim Horton … he falleth.
He standeth as Boom Boom, becometh … Monsieur Geoffrion. (laughter)
The Post … National findeth "among … academics today
McCarthy was not all bad, leastwise … in accurate…. "
He standeth as Joe Who, becometh … McCarthy. (laughter)
Namath thee WHAA—
Where's my bib. We on air?…

*

Dank pool
Player pees

Sentimental
Pis aller, all that

Velvet … spring gone
Nietzsche with it….

like "symbol."

My I
for some features

—of Place, Time, Sensation,
Thought, Event   coordinated

local excess

or for a feature
-length creature, o blissful *eek—*
freak
me!

I'm popeless!

mopless
orphic in an
anus—heads up
o stretch
the ass is
falling, readers: digest
"I was fed cars"
and you …

webbed clown on ice
wefted hums, warped the haws, buttering
rubber handles
on issues substantive
in bathrooms only
notional in living rooms
were rational (fashionable) in the cloak
room … —Did someone say *et cetera*?
I mean that Latin
remotior subtiliorque in a spiritual sense … "

KFC's QED

Father, son read
palm-sized NTs.

Bilious pigeons
gather for parable about people.

Lot of white shit.
Plenty of bread.

*

White for white, I'm abstract, expressionist—
    White
    Abstract
    Expressionist's
    Anonymous

    Bad
    Standing on
    Good
    Green gore.

A *non him, us* …

"Have to do the accent …

Denial of the Vest
'You have to have a thread
if not coat
preferably with arms.'"

In state,
quantifies.

And Mo says heard it from the Bush
vine? Oh, lord …

Rip
rip

"Why don't you ripen off?"

          Physical enactment
     stead of notional
     liberty.

… just might have

said my logos
for an eye, ear—senses of "organ"
many claim genetically non-modified

free-range, as supermarkets
their product
line—as I, this one

figure of theirs.
Monsanto eyes, inextricables.
Weed of need.

                    *

Is it just eeeeeeeeeeeeeeeeeeeeeeeeeeeeeeeeeeeeeeeeeeeeeeeeeeeeeeeeeeeeeeeeee
?

"Words care"
Terms return, earn their
letters

        christen your book (you balk)

          green blood   sword
                 's word
        Returns

          "We" is
          more than
          enough empty!

          Meaning ("we
          have x for
          that ... "?) never enough

Thrown over with semantic, drowned
the once fleet-footed—
estuary of   the confluence of the
compassionate   influence of
conservativism: the affluence
we besiege you; drain now.   of the flow of.
(No Muss [no moose] is watching.

        Gewgaws are watching!

          Kaiser's—*outstanding, sensational,*
                     extraordinary—
          craters
          exhumed to

original shapes
(Cousteauing the custodians, etc.)?

*

Sulks in silt (for silks)

Industry "guilt"—

ore

give

me!

Blam!

Dammit, planet.

Ungovernable sod
turned
through
alarm.

*

Call out, equitant,
bathosphere on term—
the egg yet.

The Sperm Thrower—
famous beaker odour
tilting action …
"such sculpture—not
on the laws
of *my*
court building.… "

May your jurisprudence flourish …

Look! no petals …

May 1st
Begonia
crawlin' ferlie!

("It's a good idea to begin writing a poem about the first of May in
November or December when you feel a desperate need for May.")

And yet boys' noises.   Clinking statues, all.

Glam hatchery

Bed of microphones, extension cables.
Ample, stark. Ample stalk—
        capital flower

                arrangement ("thanks")
                for the
                language sandwiches.
                                zucchini?—this on?

*

The flower of capital
roasted, salted

driving lost
around shining castle
on hill, eating well

past the margins

Frig them!
But, I am frigging, I do kiss them, I am going
                                    of my head …
Aië! aië! aië! My friends, I can stand no more.

Sit down.

Ludic fringe
tail
gater (fed cars) aide

moi!

                              *

The irony is humped—"Get your Gropius *off* me"

            "…to repair *through* my own flue?"
huffy

inhalation "paradiso"
about these fumes

in these rooms

to have known you, just a bit ...

puffed

—"Unleash the microscopic brain!"

A *Mastercard* on your modernism

Pulls plenty—
Your chains, your chance,
your change.

*

Mannerist vegetables

The depeopled poet
exited

When the Hegelians
pursued the battle

Dragon, dragging it on through
another galaxy.

They hardly need
keep up with our boredom anymore (etc.)

What are you going to do?

Do judges *x* sheep?

Am I bleating green?

Your teeth are sewing (sound of whirring machinery)

Jason Christie

Solvent

We had a back-to-nature weekend because our household robots went on a religious retreat. When they returned on Sunday evening, the toaster exclaimed: "I come from the sea just like you!" before it plugged itself into the socket under the cupboard. To which my wife, who has never quite trusted robots, replied: "I told you giving them the vote was a bad idea." I shrugged and had to tell the dryer later that night it wasn't allowed to sleep in our bed anymore.

VERNAL CONIFER SEANCE

This poem isn't a nation. A nation of trees pulped and bleached into something we are bound to recognize through the ink, through the words. Think through:

1. Your right to watch *The Simple Life* is a guarantee.
2. There are doors in the walls at the edges of your nation which can be locked, the blinds on the windows drawn, shutters closed, a mapped carpet covers the trap door in the living room of your nation. Only you and I know about it now.
3. This poem is not a nation at war.
4. There are no more trees in this poem.
5. The nation mourns.
6. The presidency locates itself outside of the poem.
7. The nation used to be a ritual.
8. The poem used to be a small house in the country near some sheep.
9. The poem used to be a body.
10. The nation used to be invisible.
11. Little children run around the poem playing "nation" until dusk.
12. Our lockable nation organizes around necessity, to keep the bugs outside it has screens on all the windows and doors, to keep the animals beyond what we built there are walls and fences around the nation, to keep the food on the table we spell correctly, we sleep well at night all wrapped up in our nation. Who will speak for this poem?

Neutrino (means little one)

I am three letters. You are a new phenomenon. What it is. That discord. My country
advanced the page into twenty-first century screened tamper-proof of logic: unstable
to appear there, built from "a thousand points of light," your new project: to monitor
the plateaus. In vitro estimation of language to be and just be then what is now is it.
Directly rip, it barely reacts with any form of matter. Matter (comma) words

Rosanna Deerchild

This is a small northern town

Slow coffee shop days where talk of the mine and reheated gossip are mixed into one-dollar refill, refill and refill. Then home at nickel mine shift change.

Fast country music weekends cause spill out into the street fights, break-ups/make-ups babies and heartaches. It's a country song played over and over. The jukebox never stops playing at the inn.

In a small northern town dirty pickup trucks and slow Indian cars with baseball caps at the wheel drive round and round the main drive. Girls from good families dream of Inco rich boyfriends.

There is nothing down the one highway out.

Red skins/white skins remain in sequenced order. They are beads sewn parallel on skin/lines never break to mix in exquisite disarray. Never to spill over the trees in bright-coloured chaos.

Small northern town is unmoving. Small northern town—someday I will leave you.

SNAG

on the weekends
she dances
enters into the glowing
enticed by coloured shapes
that slide
beneath her skin
like ribbons stroking
tugging and tying her gently

she is lulled
by rich sounds
of clothing that whispers
as they go by
of the silver jingles that are
wa hey heya hey
when they shimmer past

pulling her along
the endless rhythms
beat her pulse to rhyme
pumping blood so fast
through heart she throbs

she is addicted
to the full smells
of leather, sweet liquids
of skins pungent
with each other
to the heavy clouds
of blue and grey smoke
that make the air
so hazy and thick
she cannot see

she dances
drawing round the floor

sees a beauty
head held high
a wild horse
she rides alongside
becomes a sly coyote
slinking beside
into view
to smile shyly

rising body becomes the hawk
flying swooping up
down brushing gently
the prey
with winged touch
catching the glint
of a glance

low on the ground
she is the wolf
looking for tracks
already knowing
where they will lead

strutting back and forth
smiling she becomes
the fox
enticing a long-haired beauty
into a snag

she is unable
to disentangle
from this place
this loveliness
powerless to the power
she dances

ADAM DICKINSON

CONTRIBUTIONS TO GEOMETRY: COLD HANDS

Before rhombus, before scalene,
before the butterfly knife of Pythagoras,
someone fumbled with wood for a fire,
holy orders came square from fingers,
angles broke and healed in the knuckles.

Cold hands are the opposite of splinters,
the numb occupancy of belief, the outside
that sticks you from within, blood
hardening, having seemingly abandoned you,
having turned to lumber clotting the lakes.

But blood opens its star-shape
in the bristles of your joints,
in the solar reminder that, outstretched,
buffooned with cold,
every touch has five sharp points.

CRYO

Cold begins in the ears by breaking sticks,
its first small fires carefully set.

Listening cools the body, cracks glass,
broken storefronts downtown,
the mouthfuls of empty street,
the echoes that throb in those
who wake suddenly, branches
high-pitched at the window.

Listening is crystallography,
fingers over piano keys, waxwings
smoking in the mountain ash.

The cold comes in as dendrites,
as words that split like the beds of rivers
in lowlands where the sea hears only salt.

Our lips are parched in the wind.

We sleep in different buildings.

Conversations are better held with noise.

Jon Paul Fiorentino

Prairie Long Poem

i have read *seed catalogue* and *the wind our enemy* and *fielding* and still i will fail to present you with this prairie long poem because if anything they have taught me to write against this form and to be discursive and elusive and most of all they have taught me to desire each other and so to perpetuate an incestuous notion of poetry which is discreetly referred to as intertextuality.

write fragments. not full sentences. but most of all disobey all instructions toward poetry.

"son this is a modem
    this is a wordprocessor
    this is a concrete metaphor
    this is a sledgehammer"

"and the next time you want to write a poem we'll start praying" the first thing i remember about winnipeg is the king's head pub and the people I dragged there in order to sap them of poetic energy like an alcoholic parasitic hybrid of student and sociopath.

the first thing i remember about winnipeg is the womb and the poetry i radiated within while sucking on a fort garry ale and looking for a hookup.

right on motherfucker hook me up—
two for twenty-five? i love you man.

let's walk through the cinematically static exchange district and discuss the meaning of staticity and let's walk closer to our surroundings. don't detach yourself from the possibilities here in this barren city as infertile as the surrounding land yielding and yielding and yielding words.

i have been on a farm (just once) and i was disobedient—i read kroetsch again while the others engaged in a profound (mis)understanding of their immediate surroundings.

the immediacy of space wasted on me as I decided to distance myself and I became i.

aborting a landscape.

"and the next time i want to read a poet i'll start unnaming" print me oh prairie long poem with your mythological power and your subversive subnature and i will be forever ungrateful like a spoiled prairie child who has only seen history from the back seat of his parents' car, his eyes peering over the limits of the child safety window.

print me in colour, defiant and disobedient to the word "color" and the absence of you. print me canadian like an alcoholic king's head patron mouthing to the clash through the stifling ambience of menthol cigarette smoke and echoing pick up lines.

print me in technicolour as an obscure reference to my conventionally contemporary attention span and my desire spanning from the airwaves of broadcast to the incestuous, claustrophobic, surge of cable.

print me oh print me in winnipeg: home of the wholesale poet and the alcoholic.

imprint me like the inward surge of metonymy and philosophical metaphor. imprint me oh prairie long poem
        through incestuous academy
                        and frostbitten home.

MISSION STREET SONG

Take an eight-cylinder engine down to Mission Street and race the trains and lose every time. Take seven gravol tablets and wake up to ironic cricketsong and the West Nile in your blood. Place your work on your tongue and swallow slowly. Sprawl out on prairie tall grass; preserve it with your nostalgic lapses. Settle in St. Boniface; photocopy your lexicon and send it priority post to the National Library. Wake up again to Winnipeg, on Mission Street:

Listen to the song of the grey city: your entire family, the police officers, the trains, the teenaged cars, the social workers, the safe houses, the scrapyards, the playgrounds are crooning

"disrepair."

RYAN FITZPATRICK

A FINE OCCUPATION

Wide enough for sleep, poems seek
frugal material for quilting: feed sacks,
pharmacy shelves. On the back porch,
a giant index of blues lyrics fetishized.
Hymn books with lyrics halted, reupholstered,
appropriated. A scaled perestroika.
Globalization in deep harbours.

A reactionary pastoralism: self-
governance with period clothing.
Rags or overalls for factory workers.
Leninism don't preserve fabric now
loincloths ooze mule-drawn plows,
drudge dirge, trees dig through tributaries.

An auction sale; a fine arts education
cuts and sets gems, or waits
in a bank queue. Dissent is a fine point.
A net over fine hair. Is a fine occupation
useful, or is utility a fine occupation?

If classed work could exclude exploitation,
a consumer composes a fine compost bucket.
Lamp is lit, poem is written, thermostat rises.
Leftovers sit in the fridge, stock portfolio,
holes in socks, chest of gems.

Of ancient culture, absence of a closed canopy
makes sword work of bristling formulas.
Union Work or Medieval Occupation Sequences:
first, bang at nouns with verbs, then
burst into room with words blazing. Rhetorical
co-ordination of firefighting resources
that land ownership makes trade equitable;
any exchange is within a system, but

with capital, huffy aggravated sighing,
matches, catalyst in an armistice like a candle.
Whale oil lamp reduces barriers to trade; on fire.

In a Union, two children are a form
of pastoralism. Shoals in the inner city—
a small hospital controls the coal trade,
Hydro-Quebec dams, schools where pine and fir
are high-priority fuels—up to Mama Bear
to jump, broker a truce among gangs,
gas stations, stakeholders. In a lamplit cave,
where binaries spreadeagle oratory
in bad love poems instead of the heart,
threshes in poplar trees spin songs,
enough lyrics to fill an arts department,

A constitution adopted grants garbage
collection. Each flower comes as a spray;
prey in the water. Unicameral coal measures,
signs of pressurized fossils on Mars;
a sold syntagma. Barely any food or water.
Barely any social contract just
glucose resistance, maybe diabetes:
solitary familial fish taco free from food court.

A muscular procedure toward centrism, or
a ten-year republican apprenticeship. A self-help
food-for-words program supplants work.
Commanders talk straight or striate.
Will an armistice end an appetite for how atoms
come apart or empty fast food cups wag arteries
like a mace? A trowel? A prod? A way to constitute?

Even in winter, the paintings are beautiful,
landscapes with maple and birch

with a river and some frigates trampling seaweed.
Bulldozers pressure fast food into
sandstone or new oil deposits. Fossils so old
they're labour laws. Robots graze for apples.

En garde against emoticons, agricultural chemicals
potentially contact antibiotic resistance.
Lipid in the product. Pupils dilate; things
shine. A case for hallucinogens:
writing poetry. Dope makes dopey.
Pulps beautiful urns. Lecture is classwork.
Tree resists horsehair brush turn. Cut-up
newsprint across the floor a single wharf boat
drift to wailing Hammond organ, rock rock.

In the body's sea, fine linen, cilantro, and
inhaling spores seize fine china:
a Marriot occupation. Woolen socks
wash in cool water, steam rise over trees.
Tangent of a smart business deal.
Arms swing: farm. In the dark,
families graze like cattle, and pastoral
activists grade papers, lichens often form
closed mats, quietists produce food. Nearby,
farmland is politicized. Ideology limited
to canned tuna, belly-button piercing,
noteworthy art. Streetlamp camera shuts
not a career choice, but a fine-tuned machine
prints banners that form a social-welfare state.

Yet, isolationism children to death.
Ozone is a powerful anti-viral; asbestos
is conspicuous in the trachea.
Engineers hold their noses from the torch smoke.

Fishermen sit in gills and pull guts out,
a fine filet at the Keg, mint with the bill.

Syntax seeks a not candy, is produce if not
carnivalesque fast food. Traditional garb feeds
off tindersticks that may light up faster yet
burn slower than books, even paperbacks.
Will come as a spray, these lamplit huts
in goose-down comfort. Genomes begin
catallaxing questions that replicate proper
genomes. Poems imply agreement, right?
If a book turns on subtitles, then stretching
still photos to home video; lymph system filters
infection—paper is old, ink is old.

Trees are tall; they care about the wildlife that belongs.
Work is routine, worthy of burning
at semester end. Work is boring. Till, until
a sentence-level sewing machine employs
local resources and craftsmen, though
fluorescent lights are cooler and burn less coal.
Fish take away snack time; food prevents
a second global depression. Pastorals where
wildlife owns this line; underground railroad
of the mind; taken prisoner, dies from lack.

MARVIN FRANCIS

WEST NILE CROW

{there's a stage play by Naomi Wallace, called *the inland sea*: where one of the characters talks of a crow that has a sword in its wings ....)

this is kind of a wake-your-ass-up poem

[UNWRAP CROW]

I call it west nile crow

How would u like to be a west nile crow

Unemployed Son of Cleopatra

prairie crocodile attitude

invisible feather asp   funeral black

shunned by all the song birds

the last one at the carcass buffet

crow flies in the window

sublet to your ex-brother-in-law

move out the window

leave your basement sweet

no more close dancing

no more cheek to beak

everyone gives u these sniper vibes

birdsky death picks at a burger king bag

the first panhandler

on the sidewalk

crow thinks revenge from a twig

crow gangs get colour

soon we will have crow marshals

recruited from the southern bush

ramrod straight   steel-assed barrel

go west young crow

before they cancel your

west nile smile.

SITTING WITH MY UNCLE

I can recall sitting with my uncle

that west end macdonalds

watching him smoke colts

sipping yesterday's coffee

listen/talk that bush

camp story

piled on top of that

small town stony

plain jail story

pile like furs at the bay

too high to care

Of mickeys smuggled into jail

fashionable camouflage those

steel-toed cow

boyboots

stories of bull cooks

sprayed with a fire extinguisher

of cars rolling three times and back on the road and just keep driving stories that crack

in the cold that spit at the asphalt paycheck

should have written all those

stories down

sitting alone with my uncle

truck drivin' tb man

hiding him in the closet

when the cops came by

tell that story from the roof

sitting alone

fast food talking

quick no bullshit all story

all alberta north

nar dreams

hitchhiking like stomping tom

all ways on the highway

stomping like a greaser guitar

stick your middle finger out

still get a ride

stick your ass on an oil rig midnite shift twelve hours to go

up and down that red hiway

JILL HARTMAN

from *A Painted Elephant* (2003)

feet tied together

silk the stems of a bouquet

to blossom to balloon here seems

seams, pistillate here an adverb

here is a bouquet of roses

chrysanthemum

stems tied here

piteous

pithy

?

SHE UNTIES THE STRAPS OF HER CORSELETTE FIRE

breathing "elephant" a wicker

basket hangs from her dainty

hot air effects the transformation white

noise blast white

hot torch, a tap of fire

tap-tap of propane in the tank

ballooning blue sky particular to this place

as many as one hundred early tap this space

summer morning you can see your

breath sound of fire.

she still carries a torch for him—torch song

Don't leave me! All misunderstandings are

forgotten, they have already flown away!

ballooning and a bottle of

champagne a delayed valentine.

too late "early starts were never her

thing but something

about these summer mornings

gets her out of bed"

red foil hearts

inflate firmament

       belate

beguile and

  bewail her

BAROQUE EXCESS OF PIG LATIN AND

other secretes a sexual differentiation:

the behemoth of speech

be a moth

smitten by a mote, the way elephants are afraid of mice.

difference between "smitten" and "smote"

ritualize the process of seduction, the mechanics of proposition

carry a torch for Hecate's sake

Roman goddess of the underworld, a Titan, a Titian

courting language, courtly love.

drown in rose petals. red satin tongues

                              speak in

Romance

courtly language, courting love

one *woos* the other

PETITION HECATE AT THE SEAL

tank with pennies and nickels, nickel-and-diming "Lori the Seal" wishes for change,

change for a wish, chokes to death on pennies and nickels, nickels and dimes,

hundreds of wishes

  of coins

  ballast in her belly

  gags on the medium of exchange

  ragged tail flags behind

  swallow icons and

  chokes on elizabeth r.

    swishes lower & lower in a circular current of (not sea)

    water tea-brown tepid, cinder black and grey spots sable sleek

    cow eyes cloud over she's slower and slower 'til

It was a dream but she's dead in the morning.

             breaks the waves, eyes pecked.

            rust foam marks her drowned forehead

Hecate's seal   her mantilla of flies

poplar leaf revolves across mirrored skies

LOST. CHILDREN HAVE BEEN KNOWN TO

crawl into fridges and suffocate

have kittens in the dryer

empty pockets of:

crayons

lipstick

pens

change

How do you know an elephant's been in your fridge?

(footprints in the butter)

found:

pennies and dimes clink of recyclables behind the door has a porthole window and

from under the door, stale beer and wet cardboard

found:

billows Downy Spring Fresh steam by the window, pillow of warmed polar

fleece on the bench

found:

a sock on the window sill, matches, mary ann smokes for the bus, the electric

heater shudders on

found:

cloudy window worn round by revolutions of socks, shirts, lint, of buttons

coins, corners knocked off

found:

lint kittens burrowed into laundry smelling for milk, mews drowned in the

washwater and clinks from the bottle depot

CHANGE available in

BOTTLE DEPOT (WHEN OPEN)

machines emptied 2wce daily

A J UNSUBTLE SERIF H OR GEMINI A FISH OR ETERNITY IN(TERRUPT)COMPLETED

lazy eternity

names of ranches, cows

homogenized with brands

chalk on brick, hobo signs

chalk though, oh no, not charcoal not metal scrape not

paint anyway

a series of codes

ideogrammatic chalk on concrete, figurative crawl into open ended

(check under *your* doormat).

brands are iron curls, sans glass

coloured light is the touch of god

through church windows

while leaded panes of glass, colourless

& lead pipes, lead type

lead paint on iron bars at the stockyards, the zoo.

painted St. Maytag Repairman on 10th St. & 9th

avenue tracks in the snow across the lot, a tent by the elbow, a tenant

& grafitti on the railcars

steam, milk pure '50s stucco

D O N A I R   B O T T L E   D E P O T   L A U N D R O M A T
black iron, disembodied, a brand(name, downy (feathers, flakes, snow

            chicken feathers fluff the brown grass from lilydale poultry

track from the bird sanctuary,
to the chicken factory, from Blackfoot Trail
Husky truck stop black coffee in styrofoam

to Christmas lit eaves, ridges
and gutters of the Deane House
(erase the shingles, planes of the roof, snow or dark)

when the sun shines
smell 1893 ghost of malt from the brewery
& the zoo. chocolate ice cream. Old Dutch potato chips. sawdust.

THE SHY BREATHING OF THE RADIATOR. NIGHT SIGHS

my anointed knuckles, a hierophant inhabits fingertips at midnight, a greenglow
sacrifice. attracts sanguine cinnabar moths know nothing of boats, their ways, the
binnacle doesn't draw mercuric insects.

at night cannibalism's alright.

consumptive nasal whine as i ravage wild cattle at Cape Ball, strip layers like thinner

strips chairs, strips of darkness for contrast in chryselephantine mosaic of ruddy gold,

of yellowed ivory dirt in seams and creases mercury filings, fillings, gild her over with

 strips, scrap

shit splatters and dirty pens, ulcerated toes red-ink-blot stand 20 hours in shit-and-piss-soaked straw on a bad night you can smell it on her, incense dung smell, elephantine the way it bull-in-a-china-shops its way through the neighbourhood.

even the trains reek less. dogs drink anti-freeze

sacrosanct cyrillic mosaic winks, big eyes feign a sumerian fright. it's all greek to her, unorthodox church defrocked, rains gold leaf petals of meaninglessness on the parking lot.

an alarm is a truck backing up the length of 8th

french fries carcass in the straw and dirt. clumsy cuneiform, popcorn naïf

smear glyphs across the threshold of the large mammal building. palatial harem moans (om), harmonium-woeful call of peacocks across the frozen Bow

no lonely dutch elephant in a three-quarter view
no fuschia bindis allowed at the zoo

SO HARMLESS AND REGAL IN THE HIERATIC DARK

sepia strands

she makes her getaway slips

cuts her foot on the chain-link

binds it with a ragged

ribbon footprints paint

the town red, serif droplets dripped

sanskrit, a mannered script

call it style.

cachet heavy as an elephant

CLIVE HOLDEN

TRAIN PHONE SEXT

sx msg n fgy mrr:
dr trn 1% mnx,
trx 69 @ 6 fr
tran fon sxt?
-th brx wl mon
th wls wl squl
n ngns rr-
ntl,
sn tx pls!
o fk
(th gvtz @ th dr)

ANTARCTICA

if you think your town's a warm place
then please antarctica
it's as cold as your mother's tomb
here,
or your deepest fear
(that you ARE alone in the universe
and any connections you make
are just smoke or chemical foam)

if you think your town's a pretty place
then please antarctica
it's as ugly as your porous face
here,
in her beading mirror
on that hungover day you became old

if you think your town's a cool place
then please antarctica
it's as daily as a bus ride
here,
on the day you got that job
and a moment's sharp elation
turned into a ten-year groan

if you think your town's a safe place
then please antarctica
it's as dangerous as a populist mayor
here,
or colour tv,
or your mother with the bomb

and if you think your town's a smart place
then please antarctica
it's as dumb as the war
here,

or the next american president,
a weatherman,
with a diploma from sears.

BIBLICAL WINNIPEG

i've been told that a storm front
can sweep in low from the N,
swallow part of the lake
and fly on to rain fish
onto our urban streets—
i *believe* this,
because all the weather
here is biblical,
the rain falls
like bullets in bethlehem,
straight to the concrete
and bouncing back up,
all you can do is wait
helpless in a doorway,
autos pulling over,
city roads becoming red seas

then in the passing of a hand,
the sun comes back—

we've been lucky to find a home here,
but we didn't expect
that *everything* was here,
including armour-piercing rain,
pooling, guttering, coursing
and every kind of imaginable pain

CATHERINE HUNTER

TWO THOUSAND AND TWO

It's winter again, you said. It was April.
Snow was erasing the city, eliminating the surface of things.
We stood on the Main Street bridge above the broken
river, and the wind blew through me,
but I didn't fall. You removed one glove, slid your hand
up the sleeve of my coat. Under the girders of the bridge,
a flock of pigeons startled and took wing. While your bare
fingers traced the rhythm of my pulse, I saw
the pigeons rise together and then separate, fly south
to the hospital, north to the Cathedral.
Love is a division, a splitting through. I felt the cold
heat of your skin against my skin, explaining
an equation I found difficult to learn: how two
can be cancelled and cleft in two, becoming
one. You took my hand. I wanted
to move on deep with you
into winter.

It's winter again, you said. It was March.
I was remembering the night you followed me
four city blocks through a blizzard when I was angry
and mean and never wanted to speak to another man again
as long as I live I mean it so help me god, but you kept walking
one two three four blocks, a windchill factor of two thousand
and two, and every time I turned around, I saw you
coming after me. Love is simple as arithmetic, a kind of subtraction.
You followed me from Ellice to Portage from Portage to Graham
from Graham to St. Mary, and on the corner of York and Garry, I stopped
and let you reach me. Love is elementary.
A peeling down to the square root.

It's winter again, you said. It was February.
We stood on the footbridge in Kildonan Park. Skate blades
scraped and scribbled on the creek. Icicles hung

from the diving board, and in the middle of the day
I became confused, the pale solar disk so cool in the white sky
I mistook it for the moon. I saw the two small clouds
of our breathing mingle, disappear. I couldn't remember
what summer was. Winter had pared me to a sliver.
Little crystal needles laced holes in my brain.
You opened my fist. We both looked at my empty palm.
I couldn't remember what I'd been
holding on to.

It was winter again in January. Then, in December, it was winter again.
I looked south, naming the bridges between our houses: Redwood, Disraeli,
Louise, Provencher, Norwood, every steel arch of the river's ribcage
a cold blade sharp enough to clean me to the bone, and love
unmade me, took me deep into the dead of winter,
straight through its polished lens. I saw the wind
uncolour the city, the rivers buckle the land.
I saw our friends lay down
their lives, one by one, through this terrible season,
until I was numb, felt nothing except
your hand on my wrist, pulling me through.

On October thirty-first, the snow began to fall.
It's winter again, again, you said.
I looked north, because north is the direction
you come from, and north is the direction you travel
when you move away from me. Love is a kind of counting
or counting down: Norwood, Provencher,
Louise, Disraeli, Redwood. The rungs of a river as long
as winter. A river you crossed, when I was still and white with grief.
You unfolded my fingers, broke me open,
and when you had stripped me utterly
naked, you touched me again.
I fell. I sank below zero.

Now, there is nothing more that can be taken from me.
Look at the sky, darkening toward spring. The trees
that open, forgiving. The students who jump up
and down in the courtyard, clapping their hands for sheer
love of the light at seven o'clock in the evening. None of these things
can ever be lifted away—not even this weightless light,
this temporary joy. Because everything that is mine I have already given
over. Because you followed me one night all the way
to the corner of Garry and York. Because you took my hand.
You moved on deep with me
through winter.

WHAT THE VOICE SEES

When you send it out of the body to seek
the shape of the room, it knows

the measure of things, the way a blind architect
knows a building. It unfolds into the four dimensions

of the morning, every plane and angle
of the ceiling, and the curve of the ceiling, and the sound

the ceiling makes when it is still. The voice is not
a hand, nor an eye, and yet it performs for you

an accurate atlas of your place here, the precise nature
of distance between table and chair, between two lovers.

At night, when the eyes close, and the hands
let go of the day they have held, the voice moves

beyond the confines of the bed,
the cramped room in which you are sleeping.

Perhaps in those dark moments
what the voice sees

is the body that housed it, the prison cell
from which it has escaped. Or perhaps the voice,

in its sculptural intelligence, sees the world
without metaphor.

Larissa Lai

from *nascent fashion* (2005)

left the opium and myopia outside
my dark truck that stifles
that moves me risking borders
and prison in the name of protection
i truck my love
i hate my truck
i web my dreamings fine silk
all sticky
i could tack
this fine weaving
i strong my solitude but
it wells my anger i told you
not nice my teeth sharpen in darkness
i gene my fury in this shit stink
theirs my own
i piss this rank anger
these insect itches
forced entry to bloodstream
the man that leers and rubs
that dangles future business
as possibility of possibility
demo mocked by rapid privilege
of cash flow

all the exposure
unknown agent arms open
and blazing
germ in the machine
o my lovely double
elsewhere and shining
fear the manoeuvre
my biochemical package
the secret mitosis of girls
nights thick with hot paste
ancient thrall of anthrax my old
acquaintance forgot at the mere touch
down and downier
hard copy all broad and helmeted
sweet winged nike
dashes for the long needle
the anecdote
to save the grand narrative

•

SYLVIA LEGRIS

from "Negative Garden"

TONGUE GRAFT VARIATIONS

1

white white iris, blue-veined. this stillness is bloodstone, flagstone, the cold stone air winding, chamber to chamber. halfway, we are suspended—a line between heart and lung. this quickening breath; our ancient breath (each small death, an eternity; layer upon layer, leaf and vein, gold leaves patterning lime. quick prick of music)

her lungs are sorrow, heavy with whole notes and half. these empty cells, a lining of words (three tones repeating: *heart heart heart*)

2

honesty; *lunaria*: satin seed, satin pod. the moon is two half-, four quarter … note her lungs, holding still holding. she is sorrow (the full moon; the full earth). look behind her eyes. clear-eyed, she sees gem stones and gem seeds, her breath held between paper (fragile and rice, polished)

her skin? her skin is pricked with notes. looking for words we are finding song (winding slips of larkspur and larkspur, *D. consolida*, pure pure pitch)

3

larkspur; delphinium (*D. consolida*). moving closer: her hands, a prayer, broken and
falling (petals to earth, ash-white, white ash). we are looking, for words, slips. there is
primrose on her tongue, holy and wilting, white white milk (of hollyhock, *Althaea*,
that which heals: word upon word.

broken, we are falling ...)

4

flat chord; and cordate. perennial sounding, earth and eyes (transparent—see clear to the other side). *lunaria*: the moon is full (open her hand).

name her: *stigma, style, stipule*. name these days (endless, endless), and night (hands outstretched). words hang from her fingers, letters tipped (this endless fall); the moon full only of sorrow, foolish, silver ...

> *pennies on her eyes;*
> *these minor keys*

5

console her. with larkspur, delphinium, *Galanthus* (milk blooms piercing snow, white upon white. snow drops,   and petals drop; declining light). she has no words (perennial silence). words broken   into seed and seedlings (*quick, quick*

slip primrose on her tongue, these little keys, the earth pricked with sound—only with: honesty; hollyhock; her echoing lungs)

                              she has no words (sorrowful songs)

12

leaving colour; leaving   breath.

fingers   blood-damp   move earth, roots. this ground   a heart—opens
her lungs, wind-fluid. air; pools accumulating (well   her gaping heart).

emulate this   white moon, this   garden. leave it all: paperwhite, peony,
rue. this garden,   elemental

(a lament)

13

the word that ascended the summer:/flower (graft moon a thin incision, look at her, sli-

cing [*& singing*] rootstock—her eyes. periphery of a fall   *flag-*
lily precipitous; the colourless

leaf margin)

14

& burgeoning words ascending. cosmos; starwort; the moon   a tear

       in her retina. these tears: snowdrop-
       anemone;   aster;   *Rosa junonis*;

       alyssum;   *a sly singing a*

       (bleeding heart)

15

earth, critical earth

white alba, glory of snow (*C. luciliae*); cold foliage (her cold old skin ex-

foliate). snow, the glory of [*elated, she's*]; these falling words—white rays,
    ray flowers, ghosts. these cold descendants: *pale earth, pale moon,*
    nebula, this nebulous garden (this

    critical ground)

16

this garden, stone-white: starwort, star aster, wisteria (the yearning earth). this

staring   moon garden: glory of the snow, globe flower;   cyclamen (circle her
white eyes, her pale iris); white rose (magnetic; tidal pull and

      pulse [*heart-waves, blood-/heat/stricken*]);   white

      lily (*juno's rose,*
      her milky milky way)

17

Rosa junonis: milk tears;

milk petals;

this white descent

baby's breath cold a condensation   frost heaving   lungs her heart her
words ice *under breath over earth against heart against cold so cold this
hold her just hold …*

this cold orbit.   cyclamen; white circuits the earth, she's (*in audible earth*) deep
in this silence, these

absolute flowers:

bellflower (gratitude; this continuous prayer);
lily, white lily (ghost edging her eye; *stigma; stomata; her hanging breath*);
chrysanthemum (truth, only this: she is coloured blind,

struck white;   her laudable heart)

NICOLE MARKOTIĆ

"VERBATIM BEGINS WITH THIS DECADE'S HIT AND MISS."

system of high-chair government. that's still pay-for-view. we depend on mad
scientists and personal gain. notice how the ball rolls from normal to Igor. right when
a skin of ice forms on top of skin. never confuse grey with different shades of grey.
yesterday's chilling thriller today's *Jurassic Park* video. oddballs share my adjectives. so
spear through a shoulder on their wedding day to give us a ghost of a chance

earwax not the best way to recycle newspaper. remember the primary colours match
the primary directive: evolve and then squash

he really does certainly believe in absolute truth. hathaway and gumbo. order now
before the lights go out

there seems to be great confusion about who's a vampire and who's going to repair
the legs of the sofa. anything goes here as long as the insides stay *in.* no need to
panic, cuz I'm paying a professional mother to worry

yearning for equators equates Colette's collateral age

"ess" is(n't) how you spell "s." sluts put their periods inside their q-marks. sue the
government when you run out of invisible ink. kinky doesn't cut it here

"e"s haven't got a proper spelling. gusts from the north. he's British that's why not

"Try book-ending punctuation vouchers."

sometimes frozen fanta is the best way to remember moving day. you should lift from the knees. soon followed by cold appetizers and a film about jesus

say it: this time the cross won't change into jewelry. your blood leaks from the inside out; try burning sugar when it's already in the candy. you have to know how to fake laughter to make the slap convincing. go easy on the tattoos, she's limping tonight. they wanted so much more than a winnebago in the grand canyon. notice the lilt of your tongue pronouncing the second sibilant

try the mouth mould. deeply or isn't catholicism naughty enough for you?

uterus; syphilis; stem cell; leech treatment; tripod

don't wait for the transliteration, not that homophobia is out there, eh? me first, them ultimate end. does history repeat peppermint gum?

my écriture feminizes the prose back home

enclosed inside *prose* snuggles the French word for dare. enhancing the inside *poem* as oh-um. my lipstick and labial teeth—how can one tell the difference? excessively I want to know why picking up hitchhikers relates to my passport on the highway. yearly long-distance phone calls dictate no more postcards. so according to Hemingway it's a candlelighted dinner? repressed phallic objects may be closer to a penis than they appear. reverse double. eyes that see double glazed. double chocolate. even banana boats or Colette's mantra

a whistle that covers my hair-lip my pink-eye my spina bifida. and she describes how her three husbands rotate 9 x out of ten. notably while he was convalescing they printed new maps. so far the grave has quadrupled. don't bet on siblings related by porous cracks and damp earth. how could he be born in an invented country when he skimmed pages to recognize the narrator?

right after addressing the letter I phoned my mother to pick it up. put that way why not show him the transparency before spoiling the fun?

normally, they don't linger

"Repeat the capitalism of narrative."

elastics once snapped and hard buttons gone soggy lose their skill. lazily refuse to substitute for one of the men on the board game

eventually the bridesmaid is what I'll use to reach another home. enter somewhere already spoken for but still quite vacant. tempting to let in a splinter of biography. yes during the night after she'd cut off her hands I watched new skeletons composing. gallop in which way for punctuation to anticipate your reading?

gradually I decide a question mark should replace the dot. the period

definitely high school wasn't the only place to fail a driving test. to be truly subversive one had to wait till 65 or over. right now

we were *all* escorting the escort: three cheers for dinosaurs on bikes!

"Seven blind curves."

she's a man in the hat she's a bucket of air

release don't pour out the detritus of punctuation gone wild. does air escape from raisins or exclamation marks from bubble wrap? peacefully the clock ticks closer to noon than to midnight. they speak their lines then hold the caesura

all sentences promise dialogue but who will measure the margins? so what asks Fred Was—so what? that poem can be perky in the morning or exempt in the afternoon. not a bit

to not ask for directions ignores the help desk at the bottom of the escalators. sleep in. not one of you recognizes a 2nd helping as editing. go lightly and step right up. play dumb. be right back

kin knows skin

"NO SUCH THING AS A PROSE POEM."

mumbled the Cyclops. shining her black leather eye patch. her rig construction tumbled into the valley of faraway and too many. yearly postcards line the ceiling. goes to show how many pairs of boots fit into one box. x-rated continues his morning breakfast. then he read that crocodiles have no tongue. except when he looked inside there curled the rogue organ. not tied or mangled at all just limp from exhaustion and only slightly extinct

the pump was low and baby crawled out the side window. well isn't that the way we harbour hegemony? nothing could prevent this story or I could pretend these words belong to the same sentence twice as often as you watch tv

CHANDRA MAYOR

from *Cherry* (2004)

DRIVING AWAY

Bloated with snow and bulging with prefab housing complexes, swollen at the edges with townhouses, and punctuated by the nailed-up shack of the man who sells lost golf balls all summer, this misshapen city is tied up by the perimeter like a noose, like fishing line. This city is a snowy illusion pinned into position by the wet dreams of squabbling pigs in factory hog farms, by the incessant whispers of call centres, the lateral scaffolding of railway tracks, all the rusty graffiti-tagged cars marked with the caliphs of transience. The trains are pregnant with grain and other mysteries or else they are empty, another illusion. They do not speak the difference, there is no song, only clutter and clatter.

Without a car, this city is an island, a penitentiary circumscribed by orange city buses and their endless interlocking circuits, ponderous, full of disease. Downtown is the underwater grotto, abandoned pale-skinned people slipping silently in and out of the bank tower. The sidewalks are slippery with packed snow mottled with sand. I swim in and out of consciousness and I know everyone.

We are all the same person in the winter, one with an orange hat, one with red gloves. Our incestuous communal dreams rise and fall and writhe amid the thin grey exhaust of packing plants. This city is the destination of death for hogs and cows, the vortex that hungrily subsumes the debris of the prairie.

All these bridges arch hopefully over the rivers, long to be swallowed in the spring flooding, the silver kisses of fish and tree limbs, tires, and other river denizens. This city dreams of cracking ice and someone always drowns. The roads are decadent with potholes. Someone is always falling in or out and booster cables sleeping in the trunk, someone is always driving away, dreaming of Kenora, Montreal, California.

WINTER NIGHT

Leaving the university, preoccupied
with lecture echoes of dance as language,

art as survival instinct, I step
from fluorescence into darkness.

I had forgotten that winter night falls
at 5:30. I had forgotten that neither

art nor language can touch me like
this wet snow, caught in streetlights

like tissue and Christmas lights.
My art will be to meet you on the street,

naked palms pressed together, mouths
open wide with pointed tongues. My instinct

is to bear witness to new winter and cold
beauty and to each other. Snow will collect

in your hair and even passing
cars will paint us bright with headlight

halos. I will survive by dancing through traffic
on Portage Avenue with you, artists unaware,

the pounding of our feet
beyond language.

SUZETTE MAYR

WATCHING A DANCE REHEARSAL IN A CALGARY THEATRE WITH A CONCRETE FLOOR

concrete tendonitis bare floor hard muscle
tricep and elbow glute
(a pair of braids)
bare tits the most honest
little hot rocket nipples

                                                      any pain you suffer
concrete pilings heat lights melt plastic

                                                      is because of you
                        (point at bony protrusions ankles, elbows, skull)

Kamikaze spotlight spins disco ball
(fire retardant skirt. The audience will hope.)
theatre and living room disc gasoline red blue green

                                                "writing's not a holiday"
bony bursitis hips
gold valium tablet

                                          dancing with no clothes on
so cold all the actors but her wear mittens toques scarves sock-piled during rehearsal
sing along with tin cans, sauce-pan tops
bony bursitis hips
backward flip into the air into the floor

WATCHING A DANCE REHEARSAL IN A CALGARY THEATRE WITH A CONCRETE FLOOR II

dancers trace the ceiling couplets and feathers bands cat suit bird suit a woman
Birdie bounces on concrete her "what's up" gentle call of the wild over a paper plate
of potato chips a slice of garlic pickle. Peel cat food off the bottom of her bowl her
husband's girlfriend's legs built like toe-shoes digs in her backpack for a hairbrush a
condom some real estate

"what's up" with you Hudson's Bay blanket and empty apartment 38 minutes from
the theatre and counting (yellow rabbits blonde Mata Haris synthetic dream
machines) a "what's up how you doing" throwing tomatoes no longer an option
(a suspicious return address says Leonard Cohen was here)

MARIIANNE MAYS

from *(HERO)neck: attempts at a portrait*

#2, IN ALABASTER

the quiet,

    i can hear you breath   e

smooth solid   c urve of the receiver
                     bird

      arch of your breath
        a c r oss the line

clearlow   are   youthere
    i can hear youbreathe

your one syllabled throat   stir

#3, In black ink

slender line

and   han   ging
   curves
     and drops

           white parchment seeps

  shift   something shifts
pulls itself up th r o u g h yr th r o a t

ink falls through your fingers

                    like rain
                    like rain
                    like

#4, IN RED

was

the sky

             that night

   bleeding its long horizon

like a flower
like a

or was it the

narrow wooden bridge

        longest single span in the world
pulse stretching against a planked wooden
                           scale

or was it the blood
 blossoming under the pressedknife

arm extended like a spine
        like a

a crook
     ed branch

cut
       like notes
       like

plucked strings

      like

     whatisthespeed of
     whatis the s peedof   t   ime
drinkingstraightfrom the bottle
   throat glowing

   tilted back

       catches the light

DUNCAN MERCREDI

COFFEE TABLE BLUES

so you try to catch the last ride
just after last call
with three exits to stare down
and the floor moving beneath you
thinking too late
it was that last one
inhaling too fast
too many blues
playing at harry's
couldn't drag myself out
dancing in one place
eyes seeing two spaces
a double combo and a prayer
and a vision appears
drink up
drink up
and a voice says
tell them about
your coffee table blues
and pepper stood by the door
saying
just put it on the coffee table
and watching the pile rise
like magic
and the roller rolled
'til his fingers seized up
and the coffee table became
an island of green
raised by passing strangers
slipping a few leaves on the table
and the music clashed
with the breaking glass
and curses by a young woman
done whatta ya mean done

you fast comin' goin'
you ain't done yet
pants around her knees
spittin' anger at the floor
I've had bigger fingers
than that worm ya call a prick
door slamming
and we all break out in a smile
as another piece of smoke
rolls by you
and as the walls close in
and i look down
there is no coffee table
mushrooms? Sure yeah
at the brunswick
main street,
and the weekend started on thursday
with lynn leading the way
and grace, full of grace clean a table blind
shooting eight ball for a beer
stopping to watch another body
fly out the back door
tripping over the blood
on the sidewalk
a stack of beer walking into taxis after midnight
on main
heading north
with abby
who kept watch on the little people
holding up the wall
four in the morning
the coffee table sometime before too late
has not made an appearance

still covered in green
and i must've thought i could walk
then i left the street behind
finding myself
for a time surrounded by northern lights

JOHN K. SAMSON

HYPOTHETICAL

Say you wake up one morning without a language.
Taken away. Stolen by a monster from a childhood
fever for some small slight. You didn't eat your peas.
You find a pen, begin to draw a day of watching
shadows wander towards the door, of smelling the garbage and touching the furniture,
pressing your face to the radiator, walking
with eyes open, eyes closed, living without naming. Unnamed.

Say you wake up one morning without time.
That stoner's lament, "Dude, it's just a construct."
You didn't anticipate that there would be nothing
to say. No "Busy," and a sympathetic sigh to reply
to the How-are-you's that line everyday with possibility.
Crowds of helpless mutes stand beside their wrecked
cars at intersections, traffic lights pulse black.

Say you wake up one morning without a body.
You miss your hands like a dead friend.
You play their favourite songs, mourn all their potential,
what they held. Make a "Missing" poster for your heart
with a description and a photo and your phone number.
Find your ribcage full of topsoil in a garden down the street.
Transplanted yellow flowers peeking out.

Say you wake up one morning without the world.
The world leaves you for another, never returns your calls,
passes you on the street like a stranger. All you can
do is eat potato chips, cry, drink warm vodka from
a jam jar, and watch TV. The *National Geographic* specials are
especially cruel. Secrets of the Amazon. Plains of the Serengeti.
And tearing up topographical maps doesn't make you feel better.

Say you wake up one morning, or be honest,
afternoon, without your constant fear for what you have.
The season is a verb, and a window is open.

The telephone rings to the traffic and birds. The clock
is broken, blinking, you stretch beneath a single white sheet,
and the world looks like it's about to say something,
but then just shrugs.

Liminal Highway

when you fall asleep in transit
you rarely wake up much closer
to where you want to be
and you've missed the song
you were waiting to hear
coming up after the ad for a
funeral home and the traffic and weather
in a town you'll never live in

or even see now that you've passed it
in a dream you don't recall

and you know there is a word
for those seconds between
consciousness and sleep where you
have arrived at your destination
accomplished your tasks and
concurrently settled into a
big old house that needs some work
next to the funeral home
with some endlessly interesting and
kind person you love unflinchingly

and traffic is moving well
weather is fair

you think that word might be "liminal"
but you are not certain so you don't
mention it to the driver whose name
you cannot remember

though you likely know him
as well as you know anyone

and you are so weary
with loitering between here
and there then and then
beauty and function you wish
you were a three-hole punch
sleek shiny black and a
mysteriously pleasant weight
assisting children with their
school presentations while
slowly stockpiling confetti
for no particular occasion

just some average day
suddenly it is needed

Ian Samuels

ESCAPOLOGY.

my school work will twist a ribbon of the trans-canada into a gordian knot where i can spend eternity hitchhiking to and from the same point of origin, in the same truck with the same plastic hula dancer shimmying on the dash and yearning for the same distant island where her plastic hula family waits in vain for her return. the future is tens of millions of bodies in the streets of the world, but who can tell if they are singing, or dancing, or marching, or just lying there, or … maybe the future is tens of millions vacationing in rock candy mountains even while their bodies drink, and threaten, and boast, and stumble, and snort cocaine and grunt their way to pale orgasms in the still bedrooms of ratty apartments or heavily mortgaged houses and stumble bleary-eyed into morning meetings pretending everything is normal. i want to know what that eye thinks about being plastered on that pyramid, and how it must feel to be an admiral's calling card. our family has plug-and-play interfaces and a one-way ticket to the magic kingdom of cyberia, where boars walk roasted on the spit but somehow aren't quite as filling as they should be. i feel like one of a class of aspiring magicians who can't seem to get out of the 100% authentic-looking trick handcuffs that came advertised with phrases like "nothing can go wrong!" and "amaze your friends as you do the impossible!" friends are perfect fodder for "reality tv" when the stakes are life-and-death and a helicopter is circling somewhere just offscreen, searchlight tracing the silhouettes of an abandoned stage-set village whose families have obviously packed their bags and left the line of fire, probably holing up in the middle of the desert where a fifty-year supply of crazy tasty spam awaits them. there are times when low-slung lizards with eyes like gemstones—the semi-precious kind— go on patrol through huge wounds in the earth that you'd be tempted at first to think were mountain valleys, and times when those lizards stay home, channel-surfing. my mind is painted in desert camouflage, hiding from the surveyor, waiting. i sleep only when the pyramid's eye finally goes bloodshot and looks for something more scintillating. my greatest longing is trapped inside a green glass bottle, but the joke's on them—it *wanted* to be there. god is standing under fluorescents in a small tenement on the eastern seaboard, pinching himself and wishing he was real enough to put a stop to all this nonsense with a plague of locusts or a good solid flood, or something. my imagination disavows any involvement with that last sentence. boys were seen cliff-diving into krakatoa's shadow right up to the fatal moment. my clothes have carried the stains of small palms ever since. the laws we have lead a double life, solemn in daylight but going to raves and buying plane tickets to thailand when they think no one's looking. i fear what's on the conveyor belts of a distant factory, but all the same i hope there might just be a sailboat in it for me; or maybe a rocket that could put me in the eye of the moon. earning my living, the monkey i recently captured seems a little resentful, but deep down i think he knows the show must go on. my dreams have increasingly involved conversations about philosophy with billy crystal as seen in the old fernando's hideaway sketches, and i'm not at all sure whether this is reassuring or disturbing. my stomach holds at least a thousand hours' worth of swallowed sentences, but these days they want out.

NATALIE SIMPSON

SENTENCING

Faking out graciously. Fake would have numerics stop. Fog short. Fog. Short hop.

Sodden twos and threes cling string bed of growing hoard for further distribution.

A partly hidden partly able parted red. Rush a bead through beaded better half broken half a leg-shake.

Break certain through brick stands sent reason to rouse a small flag flutter.

Wings would shudder.

Arisen single syncopate. Single single syncopate.

Soon he wedded cold and striking.

He stands at barn side sing.

His turn, word burns, he break, rope sick, scald.

Sick of it, basting, he lettered.

See bending in knee or knowledge pending grip pending gather.

Thrust this. Thrift Tryst.

A must.

Form simple scintillate. Simple sin tolls.

Sax.

Sentence is a word in pieces, plastered, faster.

The reluctant two some time has a future present. Tense or tense now keen through shoulder blades dull ache neighbours.

Gone a wail thin gutter undertones gather my mouth is a-brick with feeling.

One had fearing one had felt.

I'm afraid: it's rhythm. Has tone down has two tone has tricks at the stop and the stick.

KAREN SOLIE

from *Modern and Normal* (2005)

STURGEON

Jackfish and walleye circle like clouds as he strains
the silt floor of his pool, a lost lure in his lip,
Five of Diamonds, River Runt, Lazy Ike,
or a simple spoon, feeding
a slow disease of rust through his body's quiet armour.
Kin to caviar, he's an oily mudfish. Inedible.
Indelible. Ancient grunt of sea
in a warm prairie river, prehistory a third eye in his head.
He rests, and time passes as water and sand
through the long throat of him, in a hiss, as thoughts
of food. We take our guilts
to his valley and dump them in,
give him quicksilver to corrode his fins, weed killer,
gas oil mix, wrap him in poison arms.
Our bottom feeder,
sin-eater.

On an afternoon mean as a hook we hauled him
up to his nightmare of us and laughed
at his ugliness, soft sucker mouth opening,
closing on air that must have felt like ground glass,
left him to die with disdain
for what we could not consume.
And when he began to heave and thrash over yards of rock
to the water's edge and, unbelievably, in,
we couldn't hold him though we were teenaged
and bigger than everything. Could not contain
the old current he had for a mind, its pull,
and his body a muscle called river, called spawn.

MORE FUN IN THE NEW WORLD

I lied about the shortcut, the high road,
all of it. Steered through the same recreational districts
dry-eyed and frostbit, as if on rails, and pulled up
just like that. Eight yards to the motel office, one more
to ring the bell. The ice machine means well, a grey slab
I attend with my bucket. I've been here before,
paced it off and slept beneath a sheet
forty feet from the highway. Darling,
they're tearing up the highway. When I said so long
I meant that I don't understand modern manners or the solar system
or anything. That a crucial lesson
didn't take. The new math ruined a generation. Just look
what we count on: blink of binary
operations. On check-in I find hair in the drain, a ring
by the phone, as though I'm late. Too late. At check-out
I buy more time for the purpose of making suspiciously
little noise, unable to believe a mid-sized Canadian airport
the last place I will ever see you. Come back. I'm low
on cash, downgrading, looking
at what poverty means to show me. This bed,
burned by cigarettes. The chair beside it.

To Have and Have Not

To have missed the plane. To have never fit his body
to his name, felt them click, and that slip-knot below her navel
slip. To have not taken his hand, in a strange city,
and been overcome. To have reconsidered,
and meant it. To have not returned, those missing hours
presented like a bad meal, and thought that this
is how it feels to follow night across the world.
To have not lived inside it since. Oh to have taken
the guidance counsellor's advice and become a secretary.
To have done the right thing, or the wrong one,
but with conviction. To have never read *Eros and Civilization*
and developed a theory. To have asked questions first,
or none at all. To have never gone with him to the basement
and felt his mouth upon her skin. To have worn
not what she did but instead the blouse, the white one,
that with a touch falls away. To have not felt that slip-knot
slip, his body click, placed her hand upon his hip,
and been pushed up hard against the wall.

PARABOLA

Before words, mathematics nested in the Kananaskis
Valley, calculations of upsweep and plain an ache
in the bones of crow and Cooper's hawk. Hard

science lay fossilled in the scree: evolution,
cosine, fault. We camp by a river
full of fish. It's fall.

South, at Frank, the old town lies
in the cold arms of an equation. Mass,
velocity, a mountain broken by its weight. Path

of a projectile in the sway of gravity, Pythagorean music
as the rock came down. Those who remained built again,
just west, a place that rests like a miner on one knee

staring at the stripped logic of the northern slope
as engines throttle down and the sun, a plumb
bob, drops behind the seismic ridge.

Above our tent, leaves rattle dry
as fractals in the chill. His back
a warm and perfect arch.

Earlier, a young grizzly, collared,
tracked by men with dogs, humped
through campground cul-de-sacs, caught

in a tin net of dumpsters, shithouses, the racket
of trailers, wanting out to quick water and its autumn blooms
of cutthroat trout, the western crook of the valley where the berries

are good, too hungry yet for the high country, stumped by what's
bred in. Perhaps the first season alone. Yes, we wanted him
gone. Or at least far enough up on the rise, approximately

postcard size, a view: *Distant Landscape With Bear.*
Then to sleep, bodies sweet in careless symmetry
along the curve, congruent, unconcerned

by the prospect of an elemental grunt,
the indifferent variable rumbling in
to casually cancel us out.

SCIENCE AND THE SINGLE GIRL

Initially, an unbecoming enthusiasm
for dissection. What's dead
is dead and some unborn
will stay that way. All things find purpose
in the end, even the done-for,
done-in. But when it flinched
at the pin, she dumped the earthworm out the window
to the lawns and fled. Spring robins
waddling in the grass she narrow-eyed
with a resurrected Catholic dread
that longs to love the world
for what it gives, but sees the glint
of sacrifice in everything that lives.

x is all that is denied. Not erased,
per se, for a twitchy something lies
beneath those crossbeams for which *x*s on the eyes
stand in. *y* isn't finished with this yet.
It's the question of intent. In formula
they are pregnant, chromosomal
with design, with what waits
to be realized as correct and absolute. The truth
beyond the equal sign.

.

All things being equal, they are not.
What can we expect of a triangle
that we cannot expect from ourselves? Each side
a retaining wall, holding up its end. But
an equilateral affair? Please. At most,
scalene—the short straw, long
edge, and what bears up in between. The law.
Rhombus means watch out: your house
is falling down around your ears.
Look at them, drawn. Nothing gets out
or in. Perimeters secure and air inside the smell
of zero. A circle is never getting clear
of the woods, finding only the body, again and again
a leaky approximate. Despite theologies
of equation, the protractor's gleam
and grin, it's impossible to square all angles
fair. The arc can't straighten up its game,
bails out on the curve,
while congruency rides its dreary rails
like an accident waiting to begin.

Parallel to the sensible horizon bounding
the observer's view, where earth or sea
and sky appear to meet, there is one called rational,
or true. A matter of belief in what does not
reveal itself. Brief measure of comfort, then a moment
of iceblink: *white glare on the underside*
of a distant cloud caused by reflection
from a mass of ice which may itself be too far away
to be visible. It reminds you of a man you barely know,
the discordant coast of his Atlantic
irregularities. Begin to read in topographical maps
the physical relief of him. Salinity and scar.
Rock-glacier: *a tongue or stream*
which moves gradually downwards through the action
of alternate frost and thaw. A blind valley
is *where the stream disappears underground.*
Brave west winds storm with regularity and force
while from watershed flows the variable course
of his heart. Between Capricorn and Cancer
lies the Torrid Zone, wrung and wet, never oblique
in its fevers; but nearby, the high-pressure belt
of Horse Latitudes' horrid dead-eye calms. Either way,
a long, mean solar day. *Solution is one form*
of weathering. A loss of headwaters at the elbow
of capture. Winds of atmospheric depression.
Sensual agencies wearing away the geography
that keeps you apart or together. Anticline: *see Syncline.*
Mouth: *see River.*

---

* The italicized lines are definitions from *The Penguin Dictionary of Geography*, 6th ed.

ANDY WEAVER

from "were the bees" (2005)

1.

Last night during your reading
of characteristic later odes,
my idea was of resonances between phrases:
a city cannot return anything; and *in America of course*
you don't need a word like eternity.

science is always advancing new pictures of what the universe is;
for me (although I read it along oppositions that were felt)
Marx reduces things to economies—and Freud reduces
letters in which she says *you know,*
as I came back from Mallorca and

something; they were filled with domestic scenes,
Williams's letters. Pound said, "Oh, he comes in just mad after all
hive." So the bee dance still draws me. But then we're never drawn;
each man is a law unto himself and
has to be the proposition he is.

When you're not engaged with the field,
the walking,
boy, you get screwed in the trap because
every being (and we're back to law) has its own law. if
you do not have the occurrence happening
deep, the *fact* that
you feel preside over
feeling,
of course you won't believe that
we have magic obscurities in
the expression
not "lost" but seeking other levels of engagement.

2.

The Pisan Cantos and the first books of *Paterson*
I suppose we gave
to read aloud. And then from that breakthrough
vast needs were made,
and a hatred of the word eternity.   You
planned a little book called *In Homage to Coleridge*,
with the paraphernalia of contemporary
doctoring he hated.
ideas in books; these were not bees and
beehives—the atrocity that people do in the beehive!
His dogma was
the line is moving,
every level philosophically appearing, because
often you miss its message, it was the other one; but then
any law, every
happening in letters
always brings you right to that level, because
to form
myself there's a question
I wouldn't think to ask. this is the task. We must remember
Hart Crane; come close
talking about direct
ideas of a rhapsodic poem or elegy.

3.

And so going toward a dramatic center,
he's got to have his, he's got to
feel the time. Yet I'm immensely conservative of
you, a classical example.
We got outside of our own
interchanges of language.
in straight voice, what good is
the contemporary world? I sent them off to blast
it at somebody. Of course this is in St. Elizabeth's,
in a child, in gardens where
beehives similar to the cream of the
Heraclitian God read
my early rhetoric that I was ashamed of. I came
diagramming the Now. beyond the diagram,
you ain't got no metaphysic, and
I'm convinced it ain't just one or another, there is one
tune that poets of every level conceive.
They're very awkward,
so strict about keeping to the business of the poem.
God makes all things simultaneously
obscure to *him*. The word blocks his knowing.
Open the way to a new kind of
form. So my breakthrough came

4.

The key, the shifting, is
everything, the whole thing going,
a massive conversion to understand the earth
in our own translations.
I knew well that so beautiful
language where angry
beehives watched the process.
But neither Russia nor
Heraclitus had it all
near to reciting.
The diagram, the space for
writing the great reaction was
you, and this is our beehive,
this struggling to know
the sub-dictionary meaning,
the simultaneity, the reason that there is
all this countryside

5.

Now that's the kind of thing
I'm not going to take. I'm not going
around the sun instead of the sun going around the earth.
We were mistrusted, we were put down.
A poet frequently will write the high
beautiful thing, about that I was not wrong at all.
I have never written, nor did I ever
talk about
collecting honey,
for
we share in the world.

                                        i mean,
all the women in purple
would say he isn't truly spatial. But, conceptually, he is spatial.
His books get rid of learning and yet are
endlessly creative of message. This seems to me the essential
tune of law. He may be
the syllable, the powerhouse.
who really wants to be the voice of the unconscious?
I talk about myself, about a sense that
meaning *is* because we are sitting
and the word is the place where I think it. In
times obscure,
what was your reaction to time?
What was really going on was
the poem, itself its content of ideas, embodied
co-existence of all things in it.

DARREN WERSHLER-HENRY

Ten Out of Ten, or, Why Poetry Criticism Sucks in 2003 (2003)

TEN OUT OF TEN: 1

Christian Bök—*Crystallography*
(Coach House Press, 1994)

The state-of-the-art 'pataphysical poetry project arrives on the burning wings of a bona fide literary god, one arrogant blond Canuck with unswerving Nietzschean visions of immortal grandeur, built of fierce talent, obsession with the computer and desire to fuse lyrical beauty (the stateliness of Ondaatje and the devilishness of Borges) with uncompromising and scientifically disciplined experimental poetics. The successful fulfillment of such goals bring Christian to this masterpiece of the genre, a book that necessarily taps into influences such as McCaffery and Dewdney and really little else, catapulting itself way beyond into totally focused science-fiction-based writing, intense and timeless expressions of avant-garde sensibility. Within the realms of a single volume, one can't do it all, but in *Crystallography*, Bök is clearly agonizing towards being the very best at what he does, painstakingly constructing a monument akin to Superman's Fortress of Solitude; brooding crystalline writing, blazing with Christian's feverishly intelligent (and much copied) reading style and deadly heroic riffs, while demanding peak performances from his assortment of mortal and ultimately disposable mentors and influences. The end result is a dead serious work of art, an elaborate palace of lightning-fast audiovisual inundation, an exacting but scorching piece of literary achievement full of pride and bombast, but totally to the point, aggressive and wisely anchored by the rules of poetic construction, a necessary factor in raising this above academic into such uncouth realms as kick-ass. Obscenely elegant, but always adamant in the extreme.

(original text: review of Yngwie J. Malmsteen's Rising Force, *Marching Out*)

TEN OUT OF TEN: 2

Bruce Andrews—*I Don't Have Any Paper So Shut Up (or, Social Romanticism)*
(Sun & Moon Press, 1992)

Another pleasant book cover hides what I feel is the weightiest poetry collection of postmodern times, possibly the purest expression of innovative writing ever to strafe the bookstore shelves. *I Don't Have Any Paper So Shut Up* is an insane construct of pummelling power paragraphs, nary a moment slipping out of the jet stream of Sheer Force One. No shit, every time I experience this awesome black hole of hate, I come very close to actual heart palpitations, the gravity of Andrews's relentless pound drawing all tidal tendencies into a vortex of his own lockstep, building some of the largest lines in existence on such cranium crushers as "All My Friends Are Dead," "Is There A Hyphen in Hard-On?," "Thanks To Hit You," and "Stalin's Genius." The very bloodstained crux of L=A=N=G=U=A=G=E poetry, *I Don't Have Any Paper So Shut Up* is a torrential downpour of what made *Give Em Enough Rope* such a hurtful piece of machinery. It seems Andrews alone can pull off such psychotic overdrives, making no apologies for this lyrical hideousness, knowing full well such verbal slaying is merely the spoken equivalent of the careening death howls emerging bubbled and festered from the New York industrial/jazz/noise music scene. These are the kind of sentences you dream about then can't remember the next morning, progressions so demonic, you just gotta crack a smile. I don't know, what more can I say. Andrews is in sole possession of a poetics that is about as violent as writing gets, and with each book more people become attuned to the man's legacy. Unstoppable insight: "You Do Their Own Thing."

(original text: review of Slayer, *South of Heaven*)

TEN OUT OF TEN: 3

Jeff Derksen—*Dwell*
(Talonbooks, 1993)

One of the cool things about Jeff Derksen is that it's hard to tell whether he's a genuine shit-kickin' redneck or actually the kind of good-for-nothing smartass punk that rednecks would sooner stomp all over than talk to. Regardless of bestseller status or deliberate lack thereof, along with Kevin Davies's *Comp.*, Dorothy Trujillo Lusk's *Redactive*, Lisa Robertson's *Debbie: An Epic* and Dan Farrell's *Last Instance* and *The Inkblot Record* duo, Derksen's *Dwell* ranks as one of the most consistently brilliant books produced by the Kootenay School of Writing. And of the bunch, it's definitely the most crazy from the heat, the near-unanimous fave Derksen text (his second after *Down Time*). We were damn near raised on this book and it still reads fresh today. Aside from the reflective "Temp Corp," the entire text sizzles with typewriter party action, proudly driving home kick-ass summer rockers like "Interface" and the long-striding, glorious "Hold On To Your Bag Betty"; plus chunky notebook monolith "Neighbourhood" and the book's biggest, most timeless classic, "If History Is the Memory of Time What Would Our Monument Be." Hot rockin' and brimming with confidence, *Dwell* is a non-stop road trip of southern-fried licks, the essential beer-stained 8-track soundtrack for your next Kelowna bender. Ride on ...

(original text: review of Foghat, *Fool for the City*)

T<small>EN</small> O<small>UT OF</small> T<small>EN</small>: 4

Dennis Lee—*Un*
(House of Anansi Press, 2003)

He of the nautical whiskers and breezy black aria is back in strapping emotion-bent form for what to my mind becomes the Lee masterwerk, eschewing the inflatable munster bombast of *Alligator Pie* while driving a stake through the open spiral architecture of *Wiggle to the Laundromat*. Lo and beholden to the forked twister of word and deed, Dennis and his blacklung muse have delivered a dangerous, thought-paralyzing feast, rising above *Civil Elegies* into chilling all-style-encompassed scrapemarks of the soul, the most mortifying numbers being somewhat downwinded quiet pieces like "inwreck", "names," and "hiatus," the latter braced tall and thin with an all-consuming mid-poem lacuna: "The blank where *evil* held. / The hole called beholden." Sucked back tall up with Helmet's *Meantime* as a soundtrack, I'd have to say Lee has dared to bare all with the sheerest bravery … scales, sores and her black wings, melting in vampiric sunlight with astonishing authenticity. Quite simply, this is one for the critics, genre-transcending, lyrics pliable enough to evoke Paul Celan, Bruce Andrews, and Ogden Nash licked by the punk-infuriated and Satan-spawned. Lee has finally lashed out a psychological soulstorm to match the bubbling-under apocalyptic imagery threatening to be taken deadly serious for lo these many years. Hey, wipe that smirk off your face; this *siècle* has *fins*.

(original text: review of Danzig, *4*)

TEN OUT OF TEN: 5

Steve McCaffery—*The Black Debt*
(Nightwood Editions, 1989)

One of the most formidable artistic panoramas of all time, *The Black Debt* is the tour
de force from a writer fraught with the demons of genius. One giant leap beyond a
universe wholly self-created, into detailed worlds fully incomprehensible in mere
language, Steve McCaffery traps then emanates an unwilling and vengeful muse into
the deepest, fullest, and most colourful drama of psychoses ever ventured. Punishingly
lead-poisoned or punishingly dulled by ether, *The Black Debt* is a frightening cascade
of contrasting activities, all tied with a thread of verbal dementia from a writer bent
on mutually pained destruction. Far beyond evil, this is an unearthly but man-made
and administered programming, focused on a slow erosion of thought processes.
From "Hegel's Eyes"-style noisefest "Lag," one envisions fearful glimpses of the
apocalypse, which then descends to roost on the neck through riff monster "An Effect
of Cellophane," a relentless tirade leading to an awful conclusion, Hell in a taxicab,
redemption through pummelling. (And on the cover, "Monotony Test": a rodent
better left unexamined.) The original coma of souls, *The Black Debt* refuses to move
as if heard outside of time, essentially personified as one piece, one moment, one
nightmare, yet schizophrenic, split, a ludicrously progressive, break-the-rules
outpouring of ideas from the complexity of human brains blown skyward. Forget
loving this book, as you may do with many other of your personality's black inky
building blocks; for love, hate, anger and indeed pedestrian human processes of any
kind have no seed here. View *The Black Debt* with only the cold, detached nerve ends
of your intellect. All other approaches will meet certain death in collision with an
unconceded, unrepentant, unimaginable collection of psychic machinery.

(original text: review of Black Sabbath, *Sabotage*)

TEN OUT OF TEN: 6

Ken Babstock—*Days into Flatspin*
(House of Anansi Press, 2001)

Days Into Flatspin is Ken Babstock's most formidable masterpiece to date, quite possibly and paradoxically the most moving collection of rural Canadian lyrics of contemporary times, a book written by a downtown Toronto-dwelling Newfie raised in the Ottawa Valley that soundly crushes the aspirations of all poets with the hopes of someday being the first to create that elusive perfect, quintessentially georgic marriage of formalist and post-Black Mountain styles. Karen Solie has the heart, Doug Barbour has the finesse, and Dennis Cooley is the best at making us forget all our troubles, but it takes the mighty *Flatspin* to forge it all into one devastating weapon, adding a measured dose of futility to make it really cry the blues. *Days into Flatspin* is the soundtrack for genuine red-blooded recreation, for sitting on the porch, surrounded by weeds, in the middle of nowhere, with a rifle on your lap, smoking dope, waiting for something to move. It's got the most backwoods, fog-locked, no-influences resonance of any contemporary Canadian collection of lyrics to ever really let fly, even when riding the most agonized pedal-steel jams inked to page, as gloriously evidenced on the ferociously poignant "Public Space," "To Only Occasionally Ever Actually Look," "Carrying someone else's infant past a cow in a field near Marmora, Ont.," and classic highball "Drinker." Something just smokes entire bales of ditchweed about this fiercely lonesome collection from start to finish, despite some deep-seated mellow moments ("He Considers Nihilism from Inside a Culvert") and successful attempts at less adorned, light-hearted boogie ("The 7-Eleven Formerly Known as Rx"). All segues by sundown into a time-weary violence, making *Days Into Flatspin* a major masterwerk of sonic earthtones. Best experienced in an alcoholic haze, utterly and ecstatically alone.

(original text: review of Status Quo, *Quo*)

TEN OUT OF TEN: 7

Dorothy Trujillo Lusk—*Ogress Oblige*
(Krupskaya, 2001)

The rawest, most spontaneous, and most eclectic of post-Langpo texts, *Ogress Oblige* seems to have the most enthusiasm and adrenaline; unselfconscious with its imperfections and roll-the-dice anarchy. For those who might have found the '80s-era KSW in its last throes too preachy, or (in at least one case) too melodically sweet, *Ogress Oblige* provides the antidote, with blood-curdling links to a nihilistic punk past, as punishingly displayed through the polyphonic eponymous poem, or better yet, "TOTALLY PATHETIC PHALLUS IN APPREHENSION OF CONTUMESCENT INTERFERENCE," one of the most powerful and roaring blasts of ferocity ever almost harnessed west of the Rockies. The whole lengthy quest involves an inhospitable, craggy terrain crashed by freezing tidal waves, with nary a warming emotional respite in sight. Poems such as mistresspiece "CAKES AND LAGER—AN OUTRÉ BIOGRAFIB" and the lonely "'WE'RE ALL FRIENDS HERE'—A FICTION OF UNSPEAKABLE HORROR" threaten to endear while retaining the writer's syntactic meltdown, which tears through the whole mountainous mosh. *Ogress Oblige* ultimately stands as the pinnacle of Lusk's art, a book of exploded linguistic thrash dragged kicking and screaming into the realms of human interaction, a dark mirror forcing the reader to face the inner wells of a collective's often inhospitable psyches. One of my favourite works of cascading distortion ever spattered onto paper, *Ogress Oblige* manages to reveal human truths behind its blinding blizzard of ice, perfection buried in deafening chaos.

(original text: review of Hüsker Dü, *New Day Rising*)

Judith Goldman—*Vocoder*
(Roof Books, 2001)

Pristine but jagged, maniacal but clear-thinking, *Vocoder* offers initial delvations into the machinations of Judith Goldman, passing on the SoCal bean sprouts for a sixteen-ounce New York Strip of bleeding cow flesh. From its trifurcate epigraphs (the tongue-in-cheek bitten-till-it-hurts centrepiece being Mary Shelley's "I will be a good girl and never vex you any more. I will learn Greek") through the book's thrashin' last poem ("entropy") and well beyond, *Vocoder* is indeed in your face, a much meatier collection than you deserve. Harmonies swirl in and swirl out rather than provide platform, and the riffs find Dorothy Trujillo Lusk or Brian Kim Stefans more often than contemporaries Jennifer Moxley or Lisa Jarnot, making for less of a grad school odour and more sonic wallop (viz. "the axe man cometh": "How motherfucker can I sing a sad song when I remember Zion?"). Exhilarating and perfect alternative art poems for the new millennium, nimble enough for those entertained by elegance and chops, but irreverent and spontaneous enough for the indie-rawk set ("I was born in captivity, having / fucked the right people, thick / in the France of it"), *Vocoder* is indeed food for thought, composing challenging chunks of text that will crack a smile, if not floor you, still caught somewhere between commitment to power ("dictée") and commitment to melody ("[untitled]"). Six poems, then a long silence, another five poems, another long silence and yet another eight poems, all designed to crash the processors of your mind's CD player, I guess. The crystal cogent balance between might and flight.

(original text: review of the Galactic Cowboys, *Space In Your Face*)

jwcurry—*Objectionable Perspectives*
(Outlands, 1998)

A rare perfectbound collection from jwcurry emerges full flannel as the flag for the fumbling heroes of dirty Canadian concrete, saluting before its most flammable manifestation in recent years, the baddest, crustiest miscreant of a book ever to wear the Outlands dogtag. Only John Riddell's *Criss-Cross* and Gus Morin's *A Penny Dreadful* come close to the majestic plaque-encrusted placard that is *Objectionable Perspectives*, a book that pounds d.a. levy, Bob Cobbing, Jiri Valoch, and bpNichol under a jolting metal monster mash, all creaky and cobwebbed, as our favourite hobo unhinges all over the battlefield. Saw curry read "Land Is Down" (a text inspired by, and I quote, "bpNichol, Frank Zappa, and the fucking lunatic who used to live next door to me on Landsdowne") with Daniel f. Bradley at the premiere of Brian Nash's bp biopic at the Art Gallery of Ontario (!) and will never forget how proficiently frenetic the poet read, sprawling to grab every deranged syllable in the auditorium, just levelling the place, chaos be proud. Alas, in the end, *Objectionable Perspectives* is without reserve, a thing of beauty, all mud, sweat, and tears, total annihilation, absolute Grunge in probably the truest sense of the term, with that patented photocopier rot that lived most robustedly in the guts of Bob Cobbing, and to a lesser extent, in the ongoing insane Texan outpourings of William Howe. Major facemelt.

(original text: review of Mudhoney, *Superfuzz Bigmuff*)

TEN OUT OF TEN: 10

Kenneth Goldsmith—*No. 111 2.7.93–10.20.96*
(The Figures, 1997)

All balderdash and beauty, total trope and tremendousness, *No. 111* is the ultimate
Warhol Factory full of infinitely-faceted rhymes in "er," maze-like alphabetical
syllabic progressions and plagiarism unrestrained, a budding conceptual writer's
dream, unlocking the treasure chest to cut-and-paste flights of fancy, and exercise in
keyboard digitalis and syllable counting, wayward literary discipline and mystical
wattage in the here and now. I won't even get into the meaning of the title; suffice to
say that this book is an obtuse textual explosion infuriating the writer's detractors
with renewed vigour: direct resplendent descendant of the Oulipo and Douglas
Huebler but with all the mechanics gone mad, a Sorceror's Apprentice parable for the
word-processing era. It kicks off with a manic monosyllabic abecedary—classic,
hyperbolic, heavy, all hiccups and furtiveness as Goldsmith lays down the opening
salvo. Next come the two-syllable rhymes, sandwiched together like plywood power
chords, the progressive and the sublimely melodic. Finally, in a highly informative
display that is the essence of totally unbridled verve (and nerve), all 7,228 syllables of
"The Rocking-Horse Winner," caring nary an iota for the inevitable disbelief of a
world briefly distorted by postmodernism. Hard to believe, perhaps, but I see a
certain raw, intellectual anarchy, here let loose in the hands of a player rather than a
bullshitter. Fact is, those who try to dis Goldsmith can't help but notice that *No. 111*
stands up a heap taller than anything growing out in Iowa or haunting the chapel at
St. Mark's. Hard work, no matter how misdirected, will always result in some sort of
permanence.

(original text: review of Rush, *Hemispheres*)

WARNING: Contains high levels of Obtainium

All original texts were shamelessly looted and rebuilt from reviews in Martin Popoff's *The Collector's Guide To Heavy Metal* (Toronto: Collector's Guide Publishing, 1997), aka *Riff Kills Man!* Popoff is the most OTT music writer this country has ever produced; buy his books and learn a thing or two about crafting gleeful prose dedicated to the things you love, motherfuckers.

Publication Notes

derek beaulieu
with wax. Toronto: Coach House Books, 2003.
"pronoun woven" originally appeared in *filling Station* in 2001.

Robert Budde
SOFTWARE TRACKS. Prince George: Wink Books, 2005.

Louis Cabri
"Salon, salon" first appeared in *Kiosk* (Buffalo, New York) in 2003; parts of it also appeared in *(orange)* in 2001.

Jason Christie
"Solvent" originally appeared in *Matrix* in 2005.

Rosanna Deerchild
"snag" originally appeared in *Prairie Fire* in 2001

Adam Dickinson
"Contributions to Geometry: Cold Hands" originally appeared in *Fiddlehead* in 2004.

Jon Paul Fiorentino
Transcona Fragments. Winnipeg: Cyclops Press, 2002.
Hello Serotonin. Toronto: Coach House Books, 2004.

Jill Hartman
A Painted Elephant. Toronto: Coach House Books, 2003.

Larissa Lai
nascent fashion. Calgary: MODL Press, 2005.

Sylvia Legris
Excerpts from "Negative Garden" have previously appeared in *Hayden's Ferry Review* (Tempe, Arizona) in 2002, *Prairie Fire* in 2001, and *Grain* in 1999.

Nicole Markotić
"Try book-ending punctuation vouchers," "Repeat the capitalism of narrative," and "Seven blind curves" originally appeared in *Widows & Orphans* (Nomados, 2004). "No such thing as a prose poem." originally appeared in *The Capilano Review* in 2000.

Chandra Mayor
Cherry. Montreal: Conundrum Press, 2004.

John K. Samson
"Liminal Highway" originally appeared in *The Cyclops Review* in 2002. "Hypothetical" originally appeared in *Matrix* in 2004.

Karen Solie
Modern and Normal. London, Ontario: Brick Books, 2005

Andy Weaver
Were the Bees. Edmonton: Newest Press, 2005.

Darren Wershler-Henry
Ten Out of Ten, or, Why Poetry Criticism Sucks in 2003. Calgary: housepress, 2003.

About the Contributors

derek beaulieu is a past editor at both *filling Station* (1998–2000) and *dANDelion* (2001–2003) and a special editor of issues of *Whitewall of Sound* and *Open Letter*. In addition to his magazine editing work he was also editor/publisher of housepress (1997–2004). He is the author of several books of poetry (*with wax*, Coach House Books, 2003; *Frogments from the Frag Pool*—with Gary Barwin—Mercury Press, 2005; *fractal economies*, Talonbooks, 2006) and literary criticism. His poetry and artwork have appeared extensively in magazines across Canada, and he is currently transcribing the 1963 Vancouver Poetry Conference for publication. With Jason Christie and a. rawlings he edited *Shift & Switch: New Canadian Poetry* (Mercury Press, 2005).

Robert Budde has published five books: *Catch as Catch* (poetry, Turnstone Press, 1995), *Misshapen* (novel, NeWest Press, 1997), *traffick* (poetry, Turnstone Press, 1999), *The Dying Poem* (novel, Coach House Books, 2002), and *In Muddy Water: Conversations with 11 Poets* (interviews, J. Gordon Shillingford, 2003). Signature Editions is publishing his book called *Flicker* in the fall of 2005. He edits an ezine called *stonestone* at http://stonestone.unbc.ca. He is still uncertain what he wants to be when he grows up but currently teaches creative writing and critical theory at UNBC in Prince George, B.C.

Louis Cabri's *The Mood Embosser* (Coach House Books, 2002) won a 2003 poetry book award from the Small Press Traffic Literary Arts Center in San Francisco. Recent poetry includes the chapbook *Becoming Kitsch* (Olive Reading Series, 2004). He is co-curator of the "Lineage A" poetics e-book series for Slought Foundation (http://slought.org) in Philadelphia, and of the Transparency Machine poet's context series (http://members.shaw.ca/louiscabri). Cabri has co-edited *hole* magazine and books (1990–1996), curated the poets' newsletter and dialogue series *PhillyTalks* (1997–2001), and co-edited two special issues of open letters to/from poets (in *Open Letter*). He is currently an assistant professor at the University of Windsor.

Jason Christie lives in Calgary where he likes to write about the weather and about robots. His writing recently appeared in *West Coast Line*, *Matrix* magazine, *The Queen Street Quarterly*, and *dANDelion*. He is currently not-married.

Rosanna Deerchild is a Cree poet from Manitoba's north. She is graduate of the Creative Communication Program at Red River College, majoring in journalism. Her poetry has been published in literary magazines such as *Prairie Fire* and *Contemporary Verse 2*. She has been a member of the Aboriginal Writers Collective since 1999 and has coordinated and participated in many group events. Deerchild lives and works in Winnipeg.

Adam Dickinson recently completed a Ph.D. in English at the University of Alberta. He will soon take up a Postdoctoral Fellowship at York University. Brick Books published his first book *Cartography and Walking* in 2002 and will publish his next book *Kingdom, Phylum* in 2006. He has been a coordinating editor with *The Olive* press and reading series while living in Edmonton.

ryan fitzpatrick lives and writes in Ogden, Calgary, Alberta. He is poetry editor for *filling Station* magazine. Using Google as a sail, he fishes poems from the ether that ask questions like "Why do we write?" and "Why do my shoes fit so tight?"

Marvin Francis was a Cree/Chipewyan/Urban, from the Heart Lake First Nation, Alberta, a Ph.D. candidate in English at the University of Manitoba, a member of the Aboriginal Writers Collective, a board member of the Urban Shaman Gallery, and the author of *city treaty* (Turnstone Press, 2002). He was loved by everyone who knew him and he will be greatly missed.

Jill Hartman lives and works in Calgary as a poet and micropress publisher mere blocks from where she was born. Her prairie cred is, however, suspect, since her first book of poetry, *A Painted Elephant* (Coach House Press, 2003), is narrative poetry about non-native species who romp through a millenitopic Calgary-scape and end up heading towards B.C., but she really sold out when she traveled to Toronto to be featured in the television program "Heart of a Poet," airing on BOOK TV in the fall of 2005. Since *A Painted Elephant* was shortlisted for both the Gerald Lampert and the Stephan J. Stephansson awards, she takes that as poetic license to continue writing and publishing the playful and out-of-place—pirates, burlesque, hockey, ouija. Find it in chapbooks from semi-precious press, housepress, Olive, and MODL Press, in *The Queen Street Quarterly* and *filling Station*, online in *DIAGRAM*, and in the anthology *Shift and Switch* (Mercury Press, 2005).

Clive Holden is a writer, film-maker, and artist. A native of Victoria, he now lives in Toronto. He has published several books and CDs, and his films and videos have screened internationally at events such as the International Film Festival Rotterdam, transmediale in Berlin, and the London International Film Festival.

Catherine Hunter teaches English at the University of Winnipeg. She has published one spoken word CD, *Rush Hour* (Cyclops Press, 2000), and three collections of poetry, *Necessary Crimes* (Blizzard Publishing, 1988), *Lunar Wake* (Turnstone Press, 1994), and *Latent Heat* (Nuage Editions, 1997), for which she received the Manitoba Book of the Year Award.

Larissa Lai was born in La Jolla, California, grew up in Newfoundland and lived and worked in Vancouver for many years as a writer, cultural organizer, and editor. Her first novel, *When Fox Is a Thousand* (Press Gang, 1995) was shortlisted for the Chapters/Books in Canada First Novel Award. Her second novel, *Salt Fish Girl* (Thomas Allen Publishers, 2002) was shortlisted for the Sunburst Award, the Tiptree Award, and the City of Calgary W. O. Mitchell Award. She has an M.A. in creative writing from the University of East Anglia in Norwich, England, and is currently completing a critical Ph.D. at the University of Calgary.

Sylvia Legris's most recent poetry collection is *Nerve Squall*, published by Coach House Books in fall 2005. Her other books are *iridium seeds* (Turnstone Press, 1998) and *circuitry of veins* (Turnstone Press, 1996). In 2004 she received an Honourable Mention in the poetry category of the National Magazine Awards, and in 2001 she won *The Malahat Review*'s Long Poem Prize.

Nicole Markotić teaches creative writing and contemporary literature at the University of Calgary. She has published two books of poetry, *minotaurs & other alphabets* (1998) and *Connect the Dots* (1994)—both published by Wolsak and Wynn—as well as a novella and several poetry chapbooks. She co-publishes the chapbook press Wrinkle Books, and works as an editor as well as writer in Calgary, Alberta.

Chandra Mayor is a Winnipeg author and editor. She has worked with *Contemporary Verse 2*, and is the poetry co-editor for *Prairie Fire* magazine. Her first book, *August Witch: Poems* (Cyclops Press, 2002), was shortlisted for four Manitoba Book Awards and won the Eileen McTavish Sykes Award for Best First Book. Mayor is also the recipient of the 2004 John Hirsch Award for Most Promising Manitoba Writer. Her second book, *Cherry*, is a novel (conundrum press, 2004), which was shortlisted for the Margaret Laurence Award for Fiction. It also received the Carol Shields Winnipeg Book Award.

Suzette Mayr is the author of three novels, *Moon Honey* (1995), *The Widows* (1998)—both published by NeWest Press—and *Venous Hum* (Arsenal Pulp Press, 2004), and a poetry chapbook, *Zebra Talk* (disOrientation Press, 1991). *Moon Honey* was shortlisted for the Writers Guild of Alberta Best First Book and Best Novel prizes; *The Widows* was shortlisted for the Commonwealth Prize for Best Book in the Canadian-Caribbean region and has been translated into German by Schneekluth Publishers of Munich. Her poetry and short fiction have appeared in numerous periodicals and anthologies across Canada. She currently lives and works in Calgary.

Mariianne Mays is a writer and sometime visual artist who lives in Winnipeg. Her chapbook of poetry UMBRELLA SUITES was published by JackPine Press in summer 2005. She co-edits the arts and culture magazine *Tart*.

Duncan Mercredi is a Winnipeg poet. A Cree/Metis originally from Grand Rapids, Manitoba, he dabbles in oral storytelling like it was done in the old days. He is also known as "howlin' northwind," his radio name as host of NCI-FM's *blues on sunday*.

John K. Samson drinks and sleeps in Winnipeg. He is the co-founder of Arbeiter Ring Publishing and lyricist for The Weakerthans.

Ian Samuels is a poet who lives and writes in Calgary. A former editor of *filling Station* magazine, he has freelanced as a book reviewer and cultural writer and has been heavily involved in the literary and cultural life of Alberta through a variety of festivals and reading series. His first book *Cabra* (Red Deer Press, 2001) explored nineteenth-century Brazil as seen from afar through a haze of legend, while his latest, *The Ubiquitous Big* (Coach House Books, 2004), treads the silver screen-generated landscape of popular culture.

Natalie Simpson is a past editor of *filling Station* magazine in Calgary. Her work has appeared in *The Queen Street Quarterly, dANDelion, (orange), endNOTE*, and she has written several chapbooks including *making hole* (2002) and *mount of olives* (2000), both published by housepress.

Karen Solie was born in Moose Jaw and raised in southwest Saskatchewan. She is the author of two collections of poetry, *Short Haul Engine* (2001) and *Modern and Normal* (2005), both published by Brick Books. Having tried out Medicine Hat, Lethbridge, Austin, Victoria, and Edmonton, she now lives in Toronto.

Andy Weaver's poetry has appeared in various journals, the anthology *evergreen: six new poets* (Black Moss Press, 2002), and the chapbook *not knowing spanish* (Greenboathouse, 2002). His first full book of poetry, *Were the Bees*, was published by NeWest Press in 2005. He lives in Edmonton.

Darren Wershler-Henry lives and writes in Toronto. He is fully aware that he is Part of the Problem. "And honey you can tell / All of your friends / I won't be home again / Not for anyone"—Jim Bryson, "Sleeping in Toronto"

ABOUT THE EDITORS

Jon Paul Fiorentino is a poet, editor, and teacher. His collection of poetry, *Transcona Fragments* (Cyclops Press, 2002) was a finalist for the Carol Shields Winnipeg Book Award. He is also the author of *Asthmatica* (Insomniac Press, 2005) and *Hello Serotonin* (Coach House Books, 2004) and the managing editor of *Matrix* magazine.

Robert Kroetsch is one of Canada's most beloved literary figures. He is a novelist, theorist, and poet. His most recent collections of poems include the full-length collections *The Snowbird Poems* (2004) and *The Hornbooks of Rita K* (University of Alberta Press, 2001), and the chapbooks *The New World and Finding It* ((m)Öthêr Tøñgué Press, 1999) and *Lines Written in the John Snow House* (housepress, 2002).